saving our
children
from our chaotic world

saving *our* children
from our chaotic world

Teaching Children
the Magic
of Silence
and Stillness

Pennington
Publications

Pennington Publications
PO Box 402
Dunsborough, Western Australia 6281
website: www.maggiedent.com

First published by Pennington Publications in September 2003
Reprinted in November 2005

National Library of Australia
    Cataloguing-in-Publication Entry

    Dent, Maggie
    Saving our children from our chaotic world.

    ISBN 0-9751258 - 0 –X

    1. saving children, reconnecting teenagers. 2. building emotional well being. 3. improving learning and school achievement. 4. soul based education 5. parenting. 6. boys learning 7. strategies and resources
      I. Title.

Layout & design by DesignPrintWeb
Photos: L. Thompson, K. Middleton, A. MacFarlane, R. MacFarlane

Contents

DEDICATION

I dedicate this book to my special Dad
Bill Pennington who left our physical world and his beloved
farm and family on December 1st 1994.

Thank you for instilling in me a
non-judgemental compassion for people,
a deep love and respect for Mother Earth and
the gift of a shared passion in the life long search
for new knowledge and wisdom.
Maggie

ACKNOWLEDGEMENTS

I sincerely thank all the students who have graced my doors over the last twenty six years – you have been great teachers for me. To those individuals who have helped and encouraged me over the gestation and birthing of this book. To my family and friends for their love and support – the biggest thanks of all.

Introduction

"Relaxation training can help people deal with distress. Helping people to be able to create for themselves a "relaxation response" the opposite to a stress arousal response is incredibly beneficial to one's health long term."

Daniel Goleman, Emotional Intelligence

The Magic of Silence and Stillness

Silence and stillness does have a magic to it! It doesn't matter where you find it – in your home, your workplace or your classroom, when it occurs something magical happens.

I am really excited about writing this book. Those who know me know that I can get very enthusiastic and excited about the things that concern me most. On top of that list of concerns is the wellbeing and healthy development of our children. So often in my teaching career I met children who failed to take full advantage of their abilities, due to emotional challenges and a low sense of self or self worth and values. Low self esteem is an epidemic amongst our children. Unfortunately it is not the only unhealthy and frightening epidemic that is sweeping the children of the world.

More so than ever before we are seeing:

- ❖ More violence and assaults in our schools and communities;
- ❖ More children than ever before on Attention Deficit Hyperactivity Disorder (ADHD) medication to manage hyperactivity and inability to concentrate;
- ❖ More children presenting with depression or emotional overwhelm and overload;

- ❖ More cases of sexual abuse;
- ❖ More children suffering obesity and diabetes;
- ❖ More children suffering alcohol and drug abuse;
- ❖ More children homeless;
- ❖ More children being diagnosed with mental disorders like obsessive compulsive disorder and severe anxiety disorders;
- ❖ Children as young as five who are wanting to die;
- ❖ Children as young as three on sleeping medication to help them sleep;
- ❖ An increase in childhood and juvenile crime;
- ❖ No real improvement in school retention rates for our indigenous children;
- ❖ An ever increasing teen suicide rate.

Professor Fiona Stanley, a world authority on child health, expressed her concern at a recent conference in Australia:

"Health and behaviour problems among children have reached frightening levels and a national campaign is needed to avert a looming social crisis".

West Australian, November 9th 2002

Why is this happening to our children and in such epidemic proportions?

It is the result of many factors. The ones presented are based on my experiences and perceptions only. We have moved from an old paradigm of being, thinking and living to a new, unfamiliar paradigm. Last century was the time of a male dominated world that focused on competition and the pursuit of wealth and power, whether it was financial, military, intellectual or political. Parents, teachers, doctors and lawyers were seen to be people who held unquestioned power. Others, including our children, held these people in respect and awe. Only the educated were worthy of positions of high standing. There was a deep lack of respect of indigenous people still. Another key element to these belief patterns was the strength of religion and its influence over individuals, schools and society. Women were seen as less capable and were less valued than men and, until late in the twentieth century, were paid less for the same work.

Gradually attitudes have changed. Individuals are taking more responsibility for their own lives and health. People now question everything and, due to some major disgraces within the medical and legal world, these professions are seen quite differently to the last century. People will change doctors if they are unhappy with their treatment, which seldom happened before.

In schools the emphasis has been on teaching rather than learning. Furthermore, the cognitive domain was the major focus of students; high grades were seen as the sign of a successful student and suggested good parenting and a well chosen, well run school. Those students who struggled were seen as failures. Now, schools recognise the multiple intelligence theory of learning and know that students learn in their own individual ways. Achieving outcomes that are varied is becoming the way a student's academic growth is measured. Student centred learning is encouraged and the building of emotional intelligence is recognised as part of the process.

Part of the causes of the crisis surrounding our children is that we still have parents and teachers trying to raise children using the old paradigm system of authority and power. Yet, threats no longer work. Violence and punitive punishment is not an effective deterrent. Children, now more than ever, require input into their learning and growing. **They seem to need more kindness and compassion than did previous generations.** Children respond to people who allow them to explore their own choices and give them the opportunity to make more of their own decisions, while being aware they themselves will also be responsible for the consequences of their decisions.

Children want to be the driving force behind their own learning. Many have no desire to be rich and materially successful; they want to live effective lives with quite different attitudes and ways to their parents. They are much more environmentally aware, socially accepting of cultural differences, anti-war, aware of their own responsibility for their health and wellbeing, or lack of responsibility as the case may be. **Many young people are in a spiritual void, where emptiness, a lack of meaning in their lives and disconnection from society are part of their reality.**
Then there are the simple things:

- ❖ Too many passive pastimes, from early childhood – too much TV, computers, computer games;
- ❖ Too little quality time with family – especially recreational time spent surrounded by nature and being active;
- ❖ Too much exposure to the world's disasters via the media;
- ❖ An excessively consumer driven world that conditions our

children that happiness will come from possessions rather than relationships;

❖ Too little value on virtues, especially now that traditional religion has decreased its influence in people's lives;

❖ Poor community participation in shared raising of our children;

❖ More disconnection in families, especially extended families;

❖ Poor understanding of the role of emotional intelligence and resilience building amongst some teachers and parents;

❖ A rapidly increasing 'welfare mentality'.

As an independent counsellor and educational consultant with a special interest in emotional literacy and human resilience, I am writing this book with a sense of urgency. **I know that our children's world can be made better.** I know that because I am witnessing it in some homes and schools where the emotional wellbeing of children does come first. Research has long held the belief that happy children learn best. A safe environment where differences are accepted and welcomed allows children to learn social skills as well as academic skills. Humans are programmed to be social animals. Social behaviour is not genetic. It happens through the constant interaction of humans with other humans over a long period of time.

The magic of silence and stillness is something that helps shape the developing child in a positive way. While there are many cognitive (left brain) benefits from teaching the magic of silence, there are even more emotional and social (right brain) benefits. The inner world of children today is in turmoil and the outer turmoil of the world that we have created probably contributes. I believe that children who can build a doorway to their own sense of value and worth will be better able to manage this chaotic rapidly changing world. This means children the whole world over, not just Australian children. This doorway is found on the inside rather than the outside. As explained by John O'Donohue.

> "We need to return to the solitude within, to find again the dream that lies at the hearth of the soul. We need to feel the dream with the wonder of a child approaching a threshold of discovery. When we rediscover our childlike nature we enter a world of gentle possibility. Consequently, we will find ourselves more frequently at the place of ease, delight and celebration."

Anam Cara: *Spiritual Wisdom from the Celtic World*, 1997.

So please open yourself to the magic of silence and stillness first. Then teach it to children so that they too can take it out into the world and into adulthood as a skill that sustains them during life's challenges. Teach them so that they can hold more hope, optimism and enthusiasm, and that our world can be a better place than it is now. Please teach it now, before we lose any more of our teenagers to depression, mental disorders, drug and alcohol abuse, and suicide.

CHAPTER ONE

building emotional intelligence through silence & stillness

Forrest Gump was sent on his way to Heaven. Upon his arrival, a concerned Saint Peter met Forrest at the Pearly Gates.

"I'm sorry Forrest" Saint Peter said, "but Heaven is suffering from an overload of goodly souls and we have been forced to put up an entrance exam for new arrivals, to ease the burden of heavenly arrivals".

"That's cool!" said Forrest. "What does the entrance exam consist of?"

"Three Questions" said Saint Peter.

"Which are?" asked Forrest.

"The first" said Saint Peter, "is, which two days of the week start with the letter 't'?"

"The second is, how many seconds are there in a year?"

"The third is, what was the name of the swagman in Waltzing Matilda?"

"Now," said Saint Peter, "go away and think about those questions and when I call upon you Forrest I shall expect you to have the answers ready for me".

So Forrest went away and gave those three questions considerable thought.

The following morning, Saint Peter called upon Forrest and asked if he had considered the questions, to which Forrest replied, "I have".

"Well then," said Saint Peter, "which two days of the week start with the letter 't'?"

Forrest said, "today…, and tomorrow".

Saint Peter pondered this answer for some time, and decided that indeed the answer can be applied to the question.

"Well then Forrest, could I have your answer to the second of the three questions?" Saint Peter went on, "How many seconds in a year?"

Forrest replied, "Just twelve!"

"Only twelve?" exclaimed Saint Peter! "How did you arrive at that figure Forrest?"

"Easy" said Forest, "there's the second of January, the second of February, right through to the second of December, giving a total of twelve seconds".

Saint Peter looked at Forrest and said, "I need some time to consider your answer before I can give you a decision". And he walked away shaking his head.

A short time later, Saint Peter returned to Forrest, "I'll allow the answer to stand Forrest but you need to get the third and final question absolutely correct to be allowed into Heaven".

"Now Forrest, can you tell me the answer to the name of the swagman in Waltzing Matilda?"

Forrest replied, "Of the three questions, I found this the easiest to answer".

"Really!" exclaimed Saint Peter, "and what is the answer Forrest?"

"It's Andy."

"It's Andy??"

"Yes, it's Andy", said Forrest.

This totally floored Saint Peter and he paced this way and that deliberating the answer. Finally, he could not stand the suspense any longer and turning to Forrest, "Forrest, how in God's name did you arrive at THAT answer?"

"Easy" said Forrest' "Andy sat, Andy watched, Andy waited 'til his billy boiled …".

And Forrest entered Heaven.

"Academic intelligence has little to do with emotional life. The brightest among us can flounder on the shoals of unbridled passions and unruly impulses: people with high IQ's can be stunningly poor pilots of their private lives."

Daniel Goleman *Emotional Intelligence*

What is Emotional Intelligence?

When Howard Gardner (1983) brought the concept of an emotional intelligence to light in his work on multiple intelligences it made so much sense to those of us involved in the teaching of children. Our teacher training had informed us that the cognitive domain was what we worked with – the affective or feeling domain did not concern us as educators. Many teachers found that emotions could positively or negatively influence a student and yet it remained an unknown and largely misunderstood concern.

Daniel Goleman believes that eighty per cent of our potential to be successful in life is due to our emotional intelligence and not our intellectual intelligence. I discovered in my high school classes that my ability to be kind, firm and fair won respect from students, and they changed their behaviour accordingly. It was also obvious that my classrooms were safe and friendly places where students were encouraged and genuinely cared for – even those who struggled with the three r's of reading, 'riting and 'rithmetic, or whose behaviour was known to be disruptive. This resulted in good grades for my students.

Many other staff felt I was just an easy marker, or too soft on my students, yet independent assessment always validated that the work was graded correctly. I had decided that to get the best from students I would be kind, compassionate, competent and enthusiastic both about my subject and a student's own unique potential. This approach worked for the troubled students as well as the capable studious ones. Emotions can be contagious, according to Daniel Goleman, although some contagion will be subtle. I belief this contagion is also influenced by the parents' or teacher's beliefs about a child.

Those students with low literacy hated English. Being able to teach them in a subject they were very poor at was a challenge for a teacher at any time. I always had in my room a spare pencil case and spare file paper that could be borrowed without any questions. This removed the excuse that "I didn't have my stuff, so couldn't do my work…".

I know other staff thought my pencil case plus contents would be stolen before the end of the first week. It was still there at the end of the year, probably with more biros and pencils than at the beginning of the year.

Many years later, I was stopped in the street by a tough looking 'bikey' who was covered in tattoos, rings and chains. He asked if I remembered him, and I replied that he must have grown much bigger and hairier than when I taught him at school. He gave me his name and I was able to instantly recall a small, quiet, unhappy looking boy from a year eight English class twenty years before. He had stopped me to thank me for the spare paper and biros that I had provided all those years ago. He explained that he had often slept in a park because of the alcohol and family violence in his home. My classroom was the only one he could attend where he wasn't punished, or made fun of, because he did not have his files and pens. He went on to tell me that he always tried to be thoughtful to others and had learnt this from me. Here was a good example of an emotional intelligence skill that was learned from school and was modelled without a specific intention behind it. So often we learn emotional literacy from observing it in others. **Very rarely do we learn it from a lecture.**

Howard Gardner outlined five domains of emotional intelligence. They were:

- ❖ Knowing one's emotions;
- ❖ Managing one's emotions;
- ❖ Motivating oneself;
- ❖ Recognising emotions in others;
- ❖ Handling relationships.

Have you sized yourself up with this list? If not, be honest about where you are strong and where you are lacking. Men may chuckle about 'recognising emotions in others', directing it specifically towards the women in their lives. Be reassured, it is more general than that.

Let's get back to our children: What is different today?

As our children have become exposed to so much more TV and visual stimulation than previous generations of children they seem to be less socially competent. Indeed, in the US in preschool children there has been a new condition diagnosed that is called 'tactile defensiveness'. This condition requires social workers to work with some children simply so that they can mix with other children; they have arrived at preschool with very low social skills which have created quite a few problems.

Brain research has identified a period of time in a child's development where, if they miss out on gentle, loving and stimulating relationship as with parents or pets, they do not develop the ability to be caring or empathetic. As many children are raised with both parents working, a lack of such relationships is happening more and more. This is not a criticism of working parents, or day care centres and their ability to appropriately care for children, the issue is of time and quality. Many parents are unaware of the importance of this stage of development. Indeed there is a widely held perception that children learn 50% of everything they learn in life in the first four years of life (The Learning Revolution, 1997).

Recently I spoke with a family based day carer. She is highly competent and a heart-centred woman. The relevant authorities gave her a hard time because she had ducks that roamed her yard. Apparently the authorities were concerned about the health risks of kids stepping in duck poo. Never mind the potential for building emotional doorways of learning about how to care for the ducks, cuddle their ducklings without hurting them, let alone learn how to avoid stepping in their droppings and what to do if that did happen. My own boys, when they were young, were known to chew on hard kangaroo droppings and swallow sheep poo when we took our trips to the farm. With loving guidance they were able to work out the correct things to eat. They did not get sick. Neither did they end up with a fetish for animal poo! I saw this as a normal learning experience of their childhood.

Research data as reported by Terrence Parry and Gayle Gregory in Designing Brain Compatible Learning now clearly shows that unstructured play in the natural environment is extremely important in growth and development, and the integration of the neural pathways for all multiple intelligences. It has been proven to be healthier yet with the threat of litigation and fear of child abduction fewer children are spending enough time in the outside world. There has been an enormous pressure on parents to buy the best toys for their children who spend hours in front of the TV, video, computer or a Sony Play station. Yet, the research supports interactive play with others in the natural environment – the beach, the bush, the park or the garden, rather than these expensive toys, to build mentally, intellectually and socially healthier children.

When a child is immersed in play, so much so that they do not notice time go by, they reach a place of incredible significance. Firstly it is a moment of transcendence from the ordinary world. Natural, drug free, chemical free transcendence is very healthy for later life.

Secondly, that absorption is often a clue in later life about life purpose, what is important to them. For some children the activity can be watching ants, playing nurses or maybe building in the sandpit. It has a soul connection that needs to be honoured, if not treasured. Finally, the silent search for meaning that gives such a deep and profound sense of joy and wellbeing is a human need that is totally normal. It allows a really unforced and spontaneous connection between the inner and outer world to occur. This is pure magic.

In my childhood I had a difficult relationship with my Mum. I was a highly spirited, energetic and demanding child and my Mum was not very well. I was the fifth child of a family of six, all pretty strong willed and energetic kids. To escape Mum's moods and negativity I melted into the bush. As I lived on a farm there was plenty of bush. While I was there I was free and happy. I remember having imaginary conversations and arguments with God about my life. I spent hours watching bird movements and listening to sounds. I had a cubby that was a safe haven from the world. I would sing and play for hours, then come back full of joy and lightness.

Many years later when I took up meditation I was surprised that the imaginary world of my childhood was exactly like the place I found in my meditations. I again felt free of problems, light and connected to the Divine presence as I had known many years ago. I had found a resiliency skill that helped me when life was hard and unfair. It is a skill that many children could benefit from, using it to step away from emotional pain or undue challenge.

Daniel Goleman in his book on 'Emotional Intelligence' explained the qualities of emotional intelligence. **The first two qualities are the ability to avoid being swamped by emotion and managing one's emotions.** I work with both children and adults in emotional overload and heartily agree that these are very necessary attributes of emotional literacy. They help to build another important characteristic of emotional intelligence and that is one's ability to believe one can cope with life. It is an attribute that helps people avoid a place of emotional burnout. It is the ability to manage emotions and conflicts in such a way that some form of resolution can be reached. Relaxation and silent time provide a key element to such management, by giving an opportunity to reflect on life's issues in a quiet, calm way and to allow an unrushed solution to come to mind.

So often children, and later adults, bury their emotional wounds or pain so that it just keeps building. Emotion is stored in the body as tension in the nervous system, and it takes energy from the human energy field to keep the emotion under wraps. This is one of the reasons why many depressed people are so tired and physically drained. They usually have so much buried emotional energy that they are unwilling, or unable, to deal with 'in case they get swamped by it'. Buried grief and other emotions can do this to people. My buried emotions were anger, resentment and a deep feeling of being unloved, a fear that I was inadequate. It took enormous energy to keep all that hidden, and when I finally released it I was able to use so much more energy in the true living of my life. I am now blessed with abundant energy and I am sure it is partly because I have little unfinished business buried inside of me. I have cleared and released my negative emotions and continue to spend time in honest reflection on my emotions. This time of reflection helps me to manage three more of Goleman's attributes of EQ – **namely impulse control, ability to accurately empathise and to handle relationships.** Human relationships are complex and require effort and thought to be able to manage them. The final attributes that Goleman lists as part of emotional intelligence are ones that greatly influence school performance. They are the ability to **motivate oneself, to delay gratification and to have persistence in the face of frustration.** If we could give these three out in tonic form we would probably have more successful students especially in upper secondary school! So many students are unable to motivate themselves to work hard and consistently for the two final years of school. It is not easy to commit yourself at sixteen to the possibility of seven or eight years of study with little money. Trust me on that one. I struggled big time.

Dr Paul Pearsall in his book "The Heart's Code" also explores the emotional domain and our ability to find success and wellbeing in our lives. As a psycho-neuro-immunologist Dr Pearsall has come to the conclusion from his research that we have both a brain language and a heart language. Our brain language is the one most of us are connected to because it's the way of western society. We pride ourselves on being rational, logical thinkers. Whereas, to be really well, we need to listen to the heart's language – feeling! We need to have our hearts and our brains connected.

As Dr Pearsall says, "The brain's way is to 'just do it' and the heart's way is to 'let it be."

Our heart's language is much gentler and quieter than the brain. It's just a vague whisper and we must take time to focus on our hearts and listen carefully. We need to slow down to 'hear' it, because it talks to us in the form of intuition. Most of us are racing around too fast trying to get everything done in 24 hours and this hurry mentality makes us deaf to the cry of our hearts. This supports my belief that quietness and stillness allows us to hear the heart language rather than just the brain language. He also states in his book "the brain tends to be defensive, negative and prone to hostility, but the heart's nature is to be agreeable, congenial and harmonious." Now that certainly sounds like the mis-communication that is happening in many of our schools.

Too often the brain drives our body beyond its limit. We fool ourselves – our brain says we are not exhausted; we must have that promotion; we must become a partner in the firm; we need more excitement; we need to have five TVs and several cars for happiness. Our brain tells us that when we have achieved all the 'things', we will be content. So often this is the pressure to achieve that many students suffer in our schools.

Meantime, our hearts are ailing, unfulfilled, unhappy and unsatisfied. We have a gnawing feeling of despair, or that something is wrong while our brain tells us that we'll feel fine when we do this or buy that or achieve fame. WRONG! After all, it's the heart that is reminding us that all is not well – the brain has no idea.

Tim Burns, an American education consultant who has done extensive research into the brain and the development of healthy, resilient adolescents believes that "all learning is mediated by emotion." Our school system places too much emphasis on the development of logical rational thinking to the detriment of the development of the imagination and creativity. This in turn may be helping to create emotionally illiterate adolescents who use force and violence in inappropriate situations.

Brain education fascinates students and I believe it is important to bring the latest developments of learning into our education system. Twenty years ago I brought some techniques of Edward de Bono into my classroom teaching and the difference in the thinking and problem-solving ability of students changed dramatically. This led me to keep searching for techniques that improved the thinking and learning capacity of students. Then along came the amazing Tony Buzan and his techniques really do improve everyone's ability to learn. I am a firm believer that learning how to learn and think is much more important than learning pieces of information or facts. This is one of the best changes that is happening globally in schools. NLP has many such techniques that teachers can use.

Today, we have many unruly and aggressive children in our schools. They are mini volcanos with lots of unexpressed anger and hurt inside them. Yet these emotions can be released with techniques such as creative visualizations and deep breath work. They can be released with working with sand, paint, clay, dance or energy clearing techniques taken from martial arts, tai chi or yoga, with the correct guidance. Unexpressed emotions can also be diminished and released with deep connections with caring adults who allow them to own these irrational feelings. With time and reassurance children can let the anger and aggression pass and reveal who they really are. Ideally, safe and nurturing touch, like a hug, would help complete this cycle. In my counselling room so many times I simply hold children as they explore all sorts of scary thoughts and feelings.

I often say little when children are exploring their negative emotions. I focus on REALLY hearing them, being non-judgemental and reassuring them that these emotions can be freed from their nervous system. They have felt the emotions, they were real, but they are not happening now. Helping children come to a place of closure is what their inner souls are seeking, not lots of advice, lectures or platitudes. One of my teenage clients, who had been under a mental health team before she came to me, shared with me that I allowed her to go into the 'yukky' place where she felt intense hate and rage. She felt her previous counsellors had wanted her to skip that place and talk about all the good things that were happening in her life now, or possibly could in the future. Blocked emotion is stored as energy in the body and, until it is released, it will drain a person's energy field. Until then they respond with aggression or a feeling of tiredness and inability to move, emotionally and physically.

Blocked energy can be released through physical activity. Unfortunately the present generation of young people are 'couch potatoes' to a large degree. Statistics show clearly that there are more obese and overweight children in Australia and the US than ever before, and more associated illness. Physical activity and energy burning games would also help children build social skills that could help them interact with themselves and others. I would like to develop a program where children start the day with vigorous games and a deep relaxation afterwards. I would take them in creative visualizations to a peaceful place in nature where they imagine themselves just sitting and resting. Then I would ask them to throw their worries into a rubbish bin, walk away and leave them. To finish, I would remind them that all children are unique and special, all are here for an important reason, and reassure them that they are totally lovable and capable no matter what anyone says or does to them.........This may sound so simple you may wonder if it really works. It can, and does, in homes and schools all around the world. When such programs become a familiar behaviour, with repeated use they become an incredibly powerful resiliency tool to take through life.

Nuts 'N 'Bolts

Emotional Intelligence

❖ Knowing one's emotion or feeling states;

❖ Managing one's emotions;

❖ Motivating oneself;

❖ Ability to accurately empathise;

❖ Handling relationships;

❖ Ability of avoiding being swamped by one's emotions;

❖ Belief in the ability to cope;

❖ Persistence in the face of frustration;

❖ Impulse control;

❖ Delayed gratification;

❖ Hopefulness;

❖ Blocked emotions causes tension in the cental nervous system;

❖ Emotions both positive and negative can be contagious;

❖ Emotional intelligence contributes to 80% of our potential to be successful in life. IQ only 20%.

CHAPTER TWO

benefits *of* silence & stillness *to* learning *for* life

> "Soul cannot survive in a fast paced life because being affected taking things in and chewing on them requires time. Living artfully therefore might require something as simple as pausing."

Thomas Moore: *Care of the Soul*

Silent Solo Time allows everyone to:

- ❖ Question
- ❖ Intuit
- ❖ Ponder
- ❖ Reflect
- ❖ Review
- ❖ Rest
- ❖ Process emotion
- ❖ Prepare for the future
- ❖ Solve problems
- ❖ Come to terms with the past
- ❖ Invent
- ❖ Take a break from people
- ❖ Detach from conflict
- ❖ Dream
- ❖ Find inspiration
- ❖ Find hope
- ❖ Find yourself

This is a small list of the many benefits that silence and stillness can bring to people of all ages. Silence and stillness are not illegal, nor are they fattening, so it is a wonder more people are not doing it! This chapter explores the benefits although not in the order presented above. That is a list to help show the wide reaching positives and that many of these benefits seem to be simply common sense.

Cognitive Benefits

What overall benefits do silence and stillness bring for our children? Let us begin with the cognitive benefits. The brain needs time to think, reflect, review, rest and also question any new learning. It is constantly updating its file storage system, and like any good secretary, it needs time to file away old stuff and to consider where to store new stuff. It has to 'work out' what needs to be discarded, is no longer needed.

My number three son came home from high school in his final year, very excited. Apparently his physics teacher had been sharing information on the speed of light and sound with the class. In response to the questioning of this bright class, the teacher had gone on to explore quantum physics. Well, this really extended my son's comprehension of physics so much so that in the following classes, he was unable to pay attention because his brain wanted to sort through the new information for itself. Another of his friends experienced the same shift. The brain loves new challenge and learning. However, it needs time to assimilate this new learning and re-sort the files to accept the new learning.

Quite often we can wake up at two or three in the morning and wonder why we are awake. Yet this is a quiet time that the brain can use to sort through the backlog of new learning and work problems, or to try to solve functional and emotional difficulties or issues. Sometimes during 'sleep' is the only time the mind is uninterrupted by other events. That is why it makes sense to also create quiet time during your day, to give the brain much needed time to process information. You will get more sleep! Very stressed people know well the middle of the night wide-awake moments! People processing grief often find they are awake at this time, to do some quiet grieving away from the world – in private.

Wakefulness and sleeping disorders in children are often a sign that the children are existing in a very stressed 'place' in their lives. Schools can be scary places for non-conformist children, or children who are different. The following poem captures some of the challenges of being different:

Kids Who Are Different

Here's to kids who are different
Kids who don't always get A's
Kids who have ears
Twice the size of their peers
And noses that go on for days.
Here's to kids who are different
Kids they call crazy or dumb
Kids who don't fit
With the guts and the grit
Who dance to a different drum.
Here's to kids who are different
Kids with a mischievous streak
For when they have grown
As history has shown
It's their difference that makes them unique.

Digby Wolfe

I recognize some deep regrets I have from my teaching career. One of them is that I never allowed students enough time to think, to search within themselves for their own answers to questions. I am especially regretful of my fast pace of questioning and the difficulties that must have created, especially for boys.

As English teachers, we would require students to ponder answers to questions that required empathetic responses as in a discussion on a novel. If the main character rode his motor bike accidentally into a dam, the question 'what happened?' was easy for the boys. However, the question 'how do you think he felt after he rode the bike into the dam?' was much harder for them to answer. Recent brain research now tells us that boys, and also men, need anywhere up to two minutes to be able to respond to an emotionally based question, especially one where they need to make an empathetic response. This involves a move from the left hemisphere to the right hemisphere of the brain. Girls, and woman, can switch from 'side to side' almost instantaneously. I now realize that all those boys who worked out the answer to the question would then be five of my questions behind! How frustrating and unrewarding that would have been? Maybe that explains the blank look many boys get in classrooms around the world.

"Then I asked myself (about school):
How many hours did I spend learning how my memory
works?
How many hours did I spend learning about how my eyes
function?
How many hours in learning how to learn?
How many hours in learning how my brain works? How many
hours on the nature
Of my thought, and how it affects my body? And the answer
was : none.
In other words I hadn't actually been taught how to use my
head."

Tony Buzan

From *The Learning Revolution*
Gordon Dryden and Dr Jeanette Vos 1997

More think time is important for problem solving and thinking in classrooms and at home. Learning thinking strategies early in life also helps. The rapid, visual world in which many children now live encourages frustration if problem solving doesn't happen at the same speed. I am a firm believer in teaching children thinking skills. As Edward De Bono teaches, they are extremely valuable in childhood and in adulthood. Another way is to teach children the accelerated learning techniques of Tony Buzan at an early age to improve their thinking and memory skills. The brain can work so much more efficiently than it normally does; and young children need to be taught how to think, problem-solve and explore the world with their own curiosity as much as possible. I often find children get disillusioned early if they think differently to the majority of students. Variety and diversity needs to be embraced so that our future inventors and creative geniuses can be nurtured rather than stifled and bored witless.

The brain is an amazing organ. It has over a trillion brain cells. It can grow up to 20,000 branches on 100 billion nerve cells. The brain stores information you may have no conscious memory of and we learn 50% of all the wisdom we will know in our lives before the age of four. Another 30% is in place by the age of eight. **How important is parent education so that these first years are as positive as possible?**

Many researchers are now convinced that we can absorb information more quickly and effectively when our brains are in a state of "relaxed alertness."

P 135 (*The Learning Revolution.*)

This simple statement explains why we need to help children feel safe and then calm in order for optimal learning to occur. If a child is feeling stressed and threatened it will impede their learning and poor information storage will take place.

Indeed educational kinesiologists believe the 80% of all learning difficulties are related to stress. Remove the stress and you remove the difficulties.

Gordon Stokes
(*One Brain: Dyslexic Learning Correction and Brain Integration 2001.*)

Simple breathing and relaxing before learning activities can help get children into the preferred state for optimal learning. Brain gym is fantastic for helping children prepare their brain for learning. I look forward to the day when each school will have an Educational Kinesiologist working beside teachers so that early identification and treatment of learning problems can happen as early as possible. I know some Year one teachers who do brain gym almost every day in their classrooms that report very few learning problems and everyone reading by the end of the year. Kinesiology techniques help me to identify the sources of emotional issues and kids and teenagers are pretty happy that they do not have to talk too much in their counseling session. Diffusing blocked emotional energy follows on from that and once again using the relaxed state as well as some basic NLP techniques mean that many problems and issues that are causing emotional pain or negativity can be transformed without too much questioning and probing.

The amazing brain only has a certain amount of space for new learning every day. Indeed, the short term memory has a limited capacity to process incoming stimuli; thankfully that increases with age! When the spaces are filled, then nothing new can go in..., it will not be retained. That may be why much of after-lunch school time can be boring or hard for some students. This time would be much better spent doing the arts, or with physical pursuits that need action rather than brain power. The good news is that overnight the brain grows new dendrites and there is more space to take in new learning the next morning. Maybe many students have been wrongfully growled at because they are dreaming or switched off after lunch! Their brain was filled, and they needed down time to rest and sort rather have more new learning given to them.

Emotional intelligence is helped greatly by the magic of silence where emotions can be explored and solutions found to relationship concerns. "Periods of silence not only soothe the soul but allow the associations, consolidation and imprinting needed for effective learning." (Rachael Kessler, *The Soul of Education*, p52, 2000.)

Research has also clearly found that the brain needs to down load from time to time. This means it needs to pause and have a rest. This download is not done intentionally but is driven by the brain quite unconsciously. This is a time where the brain sorts out masses of new information by finding similar associations or links in order for the information to be filed so that it can be found or retrieved again when needed. It can be a time that the student daydreams or looks as though they are daydreaming as this is a less focused activity and gives the cognitive and rational side of the brain a break. By creating down times in classrooms where students have time to relax, day dream or simply use their imagination teachers may actually increase the amount of effective learning and focus time. A joint down time can help keep all students "on line" during times of new learning or when concentration is needed instead of 30 different downloads happening randomly during class time.

Non-Cognitive Benefits

Creativity is an enormous benefit of silence and stillness. Our greatest artists, musicians, poets and writers create from their heart and soul and not their heads alone. This zone of inspiration needs the mind to be calm, relaxed, and the body to be in the background. Schools that use relaxation and creative visualization before art classes and creative writing exercises have been surprised at the depth of originality that emerges. From a transpersonal perspective, this creative urge expresses our inner world whether it be the shadow, the soul, or the confusion of the mask. Colour, sound and movement all help set our unique creativity free to fly. Consequently there are concerns that the over emphasis on the cognitive and informative component to education is adding to the alienation and disconnectedness of our youth.

Thomas Moore again states:

> *"Politicians and educators consider more school days in a year, more science, more maths, the use of computers and other technology in the classroom, more exams, more tests, more certifications for teachers and less money for art." On all these counts soul is neglected "*

Using deep relaxation exercises, teachers have found that not only are students calmer, they become more caring, and feel safer. These attributes are very important in our chaotic and violent world. The bonus is that once these states become familiar to students, just stepping into the classroom will bring these feeling states back to them. It becomes a learned response much like Pavlov's dogs. The body anticipates calmness and safety, just as the reality is that in many classrooms students anticipate fear and stress. When we feel fearful, we actually open ourselves to more fear. So, by changing the inner world, we can create a safer, less confrontational way of living for students. The human psyche is geared for survival first and then for learning and success. If there is a threat the upper cognitive processes will be unavailable to the individual. This may be the reason why troubled children often fall behind in their school work.

Creating a pathway to deep quiet within the mind and body is what we can do for our youth, as young as possible and over a period of time. This means that if they are asked to reflect on an inappropriate behaviour, they will be better able to resolve it. Making better choices is what we are helping children to work out. Telling them what is better takes away their own ability to make better decisions. Rather than tell children "go to your room and think about what you have done wrong!" Maybe suggest they go to a quiet space and think of a different more positive way they could have chosen to behave.

A doorway to the inner world is fully present in young children, through their imagination. I encourage children, and especially adolescents, to know how to listen to their inner guidance. This is the silent voice from their spirit that is constantly trying to guide them to make decisions based on love and not fear. If we could have children be better able to do this before adolescence, then they would make better decisions during their teenage years. The gut feeling that something is not right, or that it may not be a good idea…, is always present, just much quieter than the voice of the ego or the shadow!!!! I am meeting so many children who are fully connected to their higher selves and they are really angry and frustrated with other children and adults who are not!!! They can become very self righteous!!! I now value any intuition training that we can create for our children and teenagers. They think its fun and yet it can give them an excellent tool to make decisions when they are away from adult loved ones, physically or emotionally.

Teachers know that students can be unsettled after lunch due to these and many other circumstances and quiet time after lunch especially brings all students back to a state of relaxed alertness, which is the optimal state for new learning. Another benefit of deep relaxation and quiet in classrooms is that it can help settle the synergistic energy field of a whole class. Students do different things at recess or lunch time. Boys will often be very active playing sport. Girls are more likely to be very active verbally. It is possible that some students may have a conflict during the break.

*Chip Wood, founder **of The Responsive Classroom,** brought rest time after lunch to his whole K-8 school. He believed that the rest time allowed the soul to feel nourished:*

"Because it honours the circadian rhythm of children and grownups and allows them to be fully present for the rest of the day. We honour the soul when we pay attention to the sacred parts of our rhythms and bodies."

(Rachael Kessler, "The Soul of Education" 2000)

I found when I was teaching that quiet time combined with deep breathing or energy grounding brought students to the same place and intention for the lesson. Towards the end of school terms I found a ten minute nap after lunch was valued and appreciated by students as they were genuinely tired. For the upper school classes who were preparing for major exams, deeper relaxations that allowed them to see themselves as coping easily, feeling happy within themselves and performing well in exams worked really well. This mental rehearsal works for athletes and for students. In a year eight class of underachieving boys I used this strategy with great success. The boys visualized themselves taking home the best report they could imagine. This included imagining their parents' reactions and, of course, their own. They had to practise creating the feeling of success because few of them had actually experienced it at school. At the end of the term they had achieved much higher grades not just in my class but across the board. They only did the visualization weekly and so the change was surprising given that they had not achieved school success before with their reports. This visualization is included on my School Mastery CD that has been created to improve school achievement.

Visualization has a power that can be utilized by all. It is the subject of Chapter Four. In summary, the better students feel about themselves, the less stress they feel about their world and the better they perform.

With emotional intelligence, quiet time helps to avoid being swamped by emotions. The higher self is always trying to remind us of things we have forgotten, or of things we need to attend to. Making the time to take your early morning 'cuppa' outside, and sit quietly while you enjoy it, is a simple way of creating a window of opportunity for your mind to calmly review the coming day or what you managed to complete the day before. Pausing is what it is called. Simple and anyone can do it. How often have I remembered a birthday or noticed something not quite right with one of my sons while taking a little time to be still and quiet. I deepen this quietness by taking a retreat from the world from time to time. With this I take myself away from all the roles I play and simply stop and listen. Retreats get touched on again later in the book and if being by yourself makes you feel uneasy, then you are overdue for a retreat!!!!

Learning is best done in a state of relaxed alertness. It is also improved by being fun and interesting. The brain also loves to be given the right "brain food" to help it function. I have found the following help children function at their best when learning or creating:

- ❖ Water – the brain can get dehydrated easily
- ❖ Natural glucose – apples, pears and bananas
- ❖ Plenty of fresh vegetables – raw if possible
- ❖ Oxygen – through deep breathing
- ❖ Being grounded and physically present
- ❖ Feeling safe

In the chapter for teachers are some strategies to bring healthy learning into classrooms. As all parents are teachers please check out the bubbles I have made that remind children how to think well!!!! (See Appendix 14) If you haven't read Tony Buzan's books on "Using Your Head" please do so. It is never too late to learn to use it better as learning is a life long process.

Nuts 'N' Bolts

Benefits of Relaxation and Silence

❖ Builds emotional intelligence skills;

❖ Gives students a time and opportunity for rest and renewal;

❖ Allows the brain an opportunity to download or downshift;

❖ Opens the way to think more effectively, especially for boys;

❖ Encourages the practice of reflection and "wisdom in hindsight", especially for boys and kinaesthetic learners;

❖ Settles the energetic fields of individuals and then the group synergy e.g. after lunch;

❖ Creates an opportunity for creative expression;

❖ Allows the highly stressed nervous system to have a rest;

❖ Helps nurture the human spirit in our children;

❖ Encourages increased memory retention and facilitates optimal performance... cognitively, emotionally or physically;

❖ Reduces stress, confusion and anxiety;

❖ Prepares the whole person to focus on new information;

❖ Creates a safe place for the imagination to play – away from the ready-made, fast-paced and highly stimulating electronic images that bombard them daily;

❖ Encourages the practice of healthy breathing and setting intent to help in times of fear, stress and worry;

❖ Improves the home and classroom environment;

❖ Creates an opening to the Divine, or the metaphysical;

❖ Builds resiliency skills to cope with life rather than just react to it.

silence *and* early childhood development

"*The body of a child will not grow if it is not fed;
the mind will not flourish unless it is stimulated and
guided. And the spirit will suffer if it is not nurtured.*"

Rachael Kessler: *The Soul of Education*

Silence is a basic longing within all humans. Sometimes it feels like the urge to run away from the world and hide under our doona until we feel better able to meet the demands of our day. Other times it is a state we create within ourselves where we are not fully present in our body and yet we look like we are. It is also the spacey look, the distracted moment, or the place where people may say to you "hello anyone home!" At times, however, like after an unexpected change, a world tragedy or a mystical moment of awe, we need space to explore within ourselves about how we feel about it, without interruption from others. This is a time of altering our own reality and is a key quality of a highly resilient person. This time is needed to work through the experience until a way of coming to terms with it, or 'getting a grip on it', is found.

Understanding the Inner Turmoil

Unresolved problems or issues cause our brain to spend time trying to work out solutions, whether we want it to or not. The main function of the left brain is problem solving using logical thought and reasoning. The right side of the brain is more creative and intuitive, and it also likes to find solutions to concerns and problems from a different perspective. This is often where we find enormous confusion within our own heads. The 'inner critic' voice that runs uncontrollably in our thoughts comes from the ego – a part of our personality that we create in order to protect ourselves from hurt, rejection and disappointment. This is also known as the mask, and in all psychotherapy work the ego is where awareness must come to so that we can understand why we think the way we do. It is, however, only one aspect of how we interpret our world and our reality.

For now, we need to know that there is a mask, a shadow and a higher self aspect to our personality. We can get confused when we believe we are just one of these aspects as we try to interpret who we are, or how we are behaving. (See Appendix 13 – Map of Personality)

Remember that we behave according to our belief systems and if we believe we are unlovable, inadequate or flawed then we will attract experiences that validate our core belief system. We will also make decisions based on this belief system. This is the sad reason why so many people live lives of poverty, lack of fulfilment and have to struggle. They believe they are not smart enough, good enough or 'lucky enough' to live any other way. They focus on their character flaws and their unhealed facets instead of their positives. With teenagers they need to have healthy living and being modelled by adults who live authentic valuable lives.

Andrew Fuller, a well known Australian resilience expert with a special interest in teenagers, wrote the following in his book "From Thriving to Surviving"

"In a world where people rush faster and faster, work longer and longer, and laugh less and less, it is important to remember that it is our connections to other people that give meaning to our lives. It is worth reminding ourselves of the four questions asked in many forms of traditional healing.

When did you stop singing?
When did you stop dancing?
When did you stop listening and telling stories?
When did you become disenchanted with the sacred place of silence?"

(Andrew Fuller, *From Thriving to Surviving* 1998)

Disenchanted, alienated teenagers have lost all these aspects of the human spirit. Schools place less and less importance on them in the pursuit of academic excellence.

Many families and communities also place less and less value on them too. I believe passionately in the importance of these aspects of "soul" in the healthy growth and development of our X young generation. I do remember a sixteen year male student telling me after a session to help him heal deep grief over losing his mother to cancer, that the deep relaxation and connection to his inner self was better than two cones of marijuana!

Inside every child is a potential for greatness. Unfortunately we seldom tell our children this. Yet they need to hear it many times throughout those formative years. While our school system hands out accolades to the academically brilliant and the sporting champions we are unintentionally telling the rest of our students that they are a failure. So many students leave school with a deep sense of being inadequate, at a deeper level than we can ever imagine. I know this from the stories I have heard in my consulting room. It is not hard to slip further when regular pain numbing alcohol and drugs are used. I wish we could prevent all teenagers from touching, smoking and using marijuana until they are well into their twenties. I have found regular use of this drug in the early teens slows motivation for life, creates a higher incidence of depression or negative emotional states, and slows reaction time when driving or working machinery. It dulls the brain's ability to manage complex tasks and decision making and these are two key features of a teenagers' formative years. The decisions many regular marijuana users make about their schooling and their relationships are seldom ones based on hope or optimism for their highest vision for the future.

Different Learning Styles

Many school systems struggle with teenagers who learn differently to high academic achievers. The hyperactive kinaesthetic learners particularly suffer because school systems are unable to meet their learning needs to any great degree, especially if they are hyperactive too. I know this well as I was such a learner. My auditory attention span was seven minutes without activity, and that was on a good day! So, after that I fidgeted, drew, unconsciously tapped my foot, and then I drifted off. The majority of boys and indigenous students have excellent kinaesthetic intelligence and maybe this explains why they struggle to do well academically in the standard classroom system.

What kinesthetic learners do have is an abundance of energy, sometimes great physical coordination, and stamina; often they achieve far more than non-kinesthetic visual or auditory learners. They can become very gifted sports people, dancers, inventors, outdoor workers, and highly competent mechanically. These people still need quiet time in order to think, plan and manage their emotional world just the same as the visual and auditory learners. **Indeed, I would suggest that this group of learners need more training to bring silence and stillness into their lives because they usually are too active to be still for long.** As a result they can be disorganised and less able to finish long term projects than other students. Kinaesthetic students become bored easily without movement or activity. These people often exercise their tension and stress rather than search for the underlying cause. While this can bring temporary relief, in time stress and tension may build up.

With the fast pace of our world there has been a growth in the need to be busy, active or doing something. In the days before the technological advances that we have today there was much more quietness in our homes and schools. The days of radio where families gathered together to listen to radio plays and news of the world have long gone. TV has created generations of passive people who stare vacantly at the TV screens for hours. Tim Burns discovered a study where young children were put in front of a TV program that had the visuals of Sesame Street but the sound track of another program. The children watched the program just the same way they watched a normal Sesame Street program. They did not notice or react to the absurdity of the two programs that were merged. As parents we have all used the TV as a babysitter. If you have young children, please limit their time watching TV. It certainly creates a lazy brain and the brain research clearly documents that authentic, unstructured play, preferably outside builds the neural pathways for later cognitive development.

The concept of educating the whole child has been around for quite some time. Religious schools have maintained that this is what they do best. They care for the academic, intellectual, physical, emotional and spiritual well-being of their students. Government or public schools were unable to nurture the spiritual development of their students as they are unable to promote any one dogma or pattern of beliefs. The nurturing of a child's inner world comes from the people who teach and care for them, not the curriculum they follow. Values and virtues education, with relaxation and quiet time as part of the normal school life, is what brings out the best in our students. Many schools are doing wonderful things in these areas and parents notice calmer and quieter children coming home in the afternoon. If it was the intention of the whole school, them this would be most effective. The earlier it is begun, the better for the child. It then can become a way of being.

With quiet times, students have time to rest and ponder on themselves and what is happening in their lives. They have time for their imagination to run wild. Tim Burns claims that "imagination and play are antidotes to violence". In research conducted on the school massacres in America it was discovered that the perpetrators of the mass killings were essentially emotionally illiterate and had these characteristics in common:

- ❖ They were ignored as children;
- ❖ Had very little play activity as a child;
- ❖ Were of average age 13-14 years;
- ❖ Typically very bright;
- ❖ Usually overweight or underweight;
- ❖ Dad was absent or poor relationship with dad;
- ❖ Didn't know how to lose;
- ❖ Few emotional breaks or gaps between a conflict and reaction to the conflict;
- ❖ Were members of groups or 'gangs' with like interests;
- ❖ Had no fear;
- ❖ Desired to use power with violence;
- ❖ Were over-users of TV, video or computer and with a preference for violence.

Gayle Gregory, Ontario, Canada

Importance of Play

A lack of play activity has been also noted in research on adult perpetrators of serious crime in the US. Being able to play in an unstructured way is very important for a healthy brain and social development of children. In communities where parents are concerned about safety, parents should work together to allow their children to play like many of us used to when we were kids. Take it in turns to be a guardian as children ride bikes, play cricket or build cubbies. Support their play by bringing picnics along. If there is one thing I am so glad I did as a parent it was to encourage my sons to play for as long as they wanted every day. Sometimes I had to find them in the dark to bring them in for dinner! I think I did it because of my own free childhood, growing up on a farm. Luckily for me it was healthy for their brains as well as for their bodies. I know how much I enjoyed freedom from supervision and the great games played with others, especially in the bush.

Reflect on this:

I Can't Believe We Made It! If you lived as a child in the 40's, 50's, 60's or 70's, looking back, it's hard to believe that we have lived as long as we have...

As children, we would ride in cars with no seat belts or air bags. Riding in the back of a ute on a warm day was always a special treat. Our cots were covered with bright colored lead-based paint.

We had no childproof lids on medicine bottles, doors, or cupboards, and when we rode our bikes we had no helmets.

We drank water from the garden hose and not from a bottle. Horrors.

We would spend hours building go-carts out of scraps and then ride down the hill, only to find out we forgot the brakes. After running into the bushes a few times we learned to solve the problem.

We would leave home in the morning and play all day, as long as we were back when the streetlights came on. No one was able to reach us all day.

No mobile phones. Unthinkable.

We got cut and broke bones and broke teeth, and there were no law suits from these accidents. They were accidents. No one was to blame, but us. Remember accidents?

We had fights and punched each other and got black and blue and learned to get over it.

We ate patty cakes, bread and butter, and drank cordial, but we were never overweight...

We were always outside playing.

We shared one drink with four friends, from one bottle and no one died from this.

We did not have Playstations, Nintendo 64, X-Boxes, video games, 65 channels on pay TV, video tape movies, surround sound, personal mobile phones, Personal Computers, Internet chat rooms ... we had friends. We went outside and found them.

We rode bikes or walked to a friend's home and knocked on the door, or rung the bell, or just walked in and talked to them. Imagine such a thing. Without asking a parent! By ourselves! Out there in the cold cruel world! Without a guardian – how did we do it?

We made up games with sticks and tennis balls, and ate worms, and although we were told it would happen, we did not put out very many eyes, nor did the worms live inside us forever.

Footy and netball had tryouts and not everyone made the team. Those who didn't, had to learn to deal with disappointment..... Some students weren't as smart as others so they failed a grade and were held back to repeat the same grade. Tests were not adjusted for any reason. Our actions were our own. Consequences were expected. No one to hide behind.

The idea of a parent bailing us out if we broke a law was unheard of. They actually sided with the law – imagine that!

This generation has produced some of the best risk-takers and problem solvers and inventors, ever.

The past 50 years has been an explosion of innovation and new ideas.

We had freedom, failure, success and responsibility, and we learned how to deal with it all.

Author Unknown

In Gayle Gregory and Terence Parry's book 'Designing Brain Compatible Learning' the authors believed that "hands-on or concrete experiences like playing in the woods and fields without the looming presence of adults, prepared the brain for learning. What may have seemed like unstructured play had a very serious purpose". They go on to write: "When children watch TV prior to the age of six, they are doing the opposite of what their brains are required by nature to do, that is to be engaged with the real world in a hands-on interactive way." (p 30)

Too much TV watching allows the neuronal pathways that could have developed to simply shrivel up, and this is why brain researchers believe too much early TV will stunt the neural basis for learning both cognitively, creatively and emotionally. **Unstructured play allows the imagination to develop, a place where children are able to create an opening to the 'magical world' of childhood.** It is where things are wonderful and exciting for them. This magical stage of childhood development takes place around the age of four to six. At this age, fantasy stories, fairy tales, imaginary creatures like Father Christmas and the Tooth Fairy, and creative activities like playing dress-ups can greatly expand the child's neuronal pathways. As well, they build an understanding of archetypes that are part of all life journeys.

Archetypes help individuals to understand life. In adulthood we are more insightful and have a capacity to reflect and question ourselves and our behaviours. As a transpersonal therapist, deep understanding and awareness of the whole person is often achieved through exploring the working of the symbolic as well as the factual or real realms. This means that we explore our inner world through examining dreams, life steps and transitions, life metaphors and our life stories as well as working closely with the body and the mind, and the spirit.

Children who experience little stimulation in fantasy can become disillusioned with life when they reach school and get down to serious learning. In my experience, children younger than ten who expressed they wanted to die all had a very limited magical child stage of their lives. Interestingly, some of these children were the children of academics who believed that teaching their child to read before school and to become "mini encyclopaedias" was far more important than expanding their creativity. Sadly they were doing what they believed to be the best for their children.

Let our children be children for as long as possible. Keep them away from news programs, advertisements that condition their perceptions, sexually explicit movies and scary movies. Our children are so sensitive to major emotional damage from viewing these types of programs. I have worked with some children for up to twelve months to free irrational fears that have been created by watching movies like 'Scream'. So, be vigilant.

Absorbed play in what they are doing is pure magic for a child. It is a mini transcendent moment that opens the child to a beautiful experience that they have created for themselves. It doesn't matter if the child is in the sandpit, hidden in a cubby, or in the midst of an imaginary activity in your lounge room, please do not interrupt them. Transcendence is a state we all enjoy. If we can find it without chemicals and drugs then we are really lucky. Many teenagers speak of seeking this state via drugs or alcohol. Deep relaxation and absorption in something creative or interesting is a peak experience. If children can find and recognise this experience early in their life there is a better chance that they will be able to find it later in life, naturally. Their parents' modelling that state for them is also very beneficial.

Nuts 'N 'Bolts

The healthy early development of our children includes:

❖ Unstructured play in a natural environment;

❖ Building a strong connection to nature;

❖ Quiet time alone;

❖ Quiet times with caring adults;

❖ Beginning short visualizations where appropriate;

❖ As little TV and passive visual activity as possible;

❖ Lots of reassurance that all children are special and learn differently;

❖ Lots of magical stimulation, imaginary games and play, before six years of age;

❖ NO inappropriate TV programs or videos;

❖ Lots of play with other children and without too much parental supervision;

❖ Lots of reassurance that they are loved;

❖ Lots of stories and play activity with parents;

❖ Lots of safe touch – head, foot, forehead massages;

❖ Time to learn how to love and care for pets;

❖ An opening to prayer or the understanding of something mysterious that is more powerful than self.

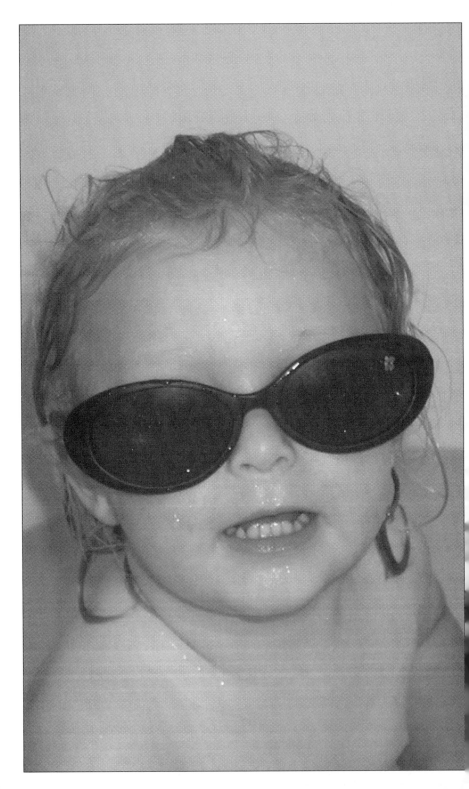

the power of visualization

*"I had amazing results on my daughter with a visualization
exercise the day after your seminar. She has been trying to
do the splits for the whole year and she was almost there. I
guided her through a visualization of her doing the splits and
then when she attempted it for real she did it easily!
Incredible and amazing stuff."*

B. Bulley 2002

Mental rehearsal has been around for years. Peak athletes and
performers have been using it for ages. How is it then that we are not
been teaching our children the true power of this activity?

I am deeply grateful to Jack Canfield for teaching the power of
visualization to me by taking me through many exercises using the
imagination. My educated brain may have refused to believe the
power because, at the time, it filtered all experiences through the
educated mind set of "where is the proof and the research to support
your hypothesis?" There is a summary of the benefits of creative
visualization as explored by Jack Canfield in Appendix 9.

I believe we haven't been teaching our children this art because it was difficult to prove the benefit of mental rehearsal was real. The sceptical analytical minds of educators and the educated thus dismissed it as being dubious. Thankfully the area of brain and mind research has been growing exponentially over the last ten years leading to the acceptance of visualization as well as prayer (Larry Dossey, *Healing Words*). The amazing results achieved using the language patterns and visualization techniques of Neuro Linguistic Programming (NLP) continue to astound traditional psychologists and those in the medical world. There are times in my work that I had to suspend my conscious understanding of how people could so successfully transform negative behaviour and performance with these techniques because the permanent changes in behaviour happened so quickly and painlessly.

The following exercise can help you understand the power of visualization from a perspective deep within yourself. It works best if you can prop your book up so that your hands are free.

Visualization Exercise

Stand with your feet comfortably apart a little. Keep your feet still during this activity as it will require you to turn from the waist. I encourage you not to force any movement, just do what feels comfortable for you.

Raise your left arm straight out in front of you. Turn slowly to the left leading with your arm, to as far as is comfortable for you. When you get to that point allow your eyes to observe whatever your hand or fingers are pointing towards. Make a mental note of that point; this is point one.

Then, without moving your arm, visually line up a different point that is further in the direction you were turning toward. Take a mental picture of this point; this is point two.

Slowly untwist as you bring your arm back to the front. Put it by your side.

Now close your eyes. Imagine you are repeating the exercise. Imagine lifting your left arm up and turning slowly to point one. Effortlessly pass that point to line your arm up to the second point that was almost behind you, at point two. It is easy, your body feels comfortable and you find yourself lined up to a place which is much further around than you were first able to turn. Imagine bringing your arm back to the front, and slowly to your side.

Open your eyes and actually do the exercise. Where does your arm now face? Is it at point one or nearer to point two? Most of you will find you have easily lined up to point two.

(Jack Canfield FSS 1998 Santa Barbara Cal, USA)

What does this visualization exercise show? It is not meant to demonstrate how inflexible some of us are – but rather that we can change our performance easily when we change our inner perception. If we can see something with the mind then the chances are much better that the body will follow. **Our brain cannot distinguish between real or imagined images. This is the key to the power of visualization.**

Albert Einstein believed that "Imagination is more important than knowledge." A healthy imagination that is encouraged and brought forward from early childhood is important. People can then imagine with enthusiasm and creativity. If you sit in a chair right now and imagine flying in a small plane at 20,000 feet, you are sitting in a comfortable seat with your seatbelt on. Chances are your body starts to feel little sensations as if you really are flying. Now imagine you are at the back of the plane and are ready to jump with a parachute through an open door. My Dad used to always wonder at why anyone would want to leap out of a perfectly good aeroplane but imagine you can feel the rush of air whizzing past you. You can see how far down the ground is, you can feel the equipment in your hands. You again start to feel body sensations – if you are afraid of heights you will feel your heart start to race, butterflies in the stomach and the palms of your hands becoming sweaty; or you may feel exhilaration.

Some people feel anxious in small spaces and have the same body sensations if they imagine themselves in such a space. The body physiology follows our mind and whatever we imagine.

Transforming Negative Behaviour

Using NLP in behavioural therapy can be really beneficial as it helps a person to disconnect from a well known pattern that no longer serves them positively. One such technique helps people with long-term depression by identifying their normal thinking and triggering sensory pathways that leads them to feel miserable, depressed and lethargic. They can learn to divert from that 'doorway'. There are many excellent opportunities to manage negative thoughts and the states that these negative thoughts create. Daniel Goleman (*Emotional Intelligence* 1996) discovered that pessimism and despair are learned behaviours, hope and optimism are also learned. We would all like to help our children learn the latter.

There is a true story in the second of the Chicken Soup for the Soul books by Jack Canfield and Mark Victor Hansen. It is about a Vietnam prisoner of war, a Major James Nesmeth, who spent seven years as a prisoner imagining he was playing eighteen holes of golf on his home golf course. Every day he would play, stroke by stroke while actually being imprisoned in a cage. In this way he kept his mind distracted from his daily discomfort and was able to keep going. Eventually, when he was rescued and able to return home, when he played his first real game of golf he had shaved twenty strokes off his previous golf score.

There is also an often quoted experiment with a group of young basketballers. They were divided into three groups. One group practised everyday over a three month period. Another group did no training while the third group mentally practised every day. The results showed conclusively that the third group improved almost as much as the first group, without even touching a basketball.

Can you see the implications for kids at schools who are underachieving? Can you see the implications for the isolated child with few social skills? Can you even see the possible benefits for creating the potential for a peaceful world one day? When I returned from Jack Canfield's Facilitating Skills Seminar training program in 1998 I felt more confident about bringing creative visualization into my classes as I was no longer a stranger to the concept.

Previously over a seven year period I had run relaxation and meditation classes for teenagers and women and knew how well they could work. What changed after Jack's program was allowing the work to take a step further. Visualization enables us to imagine ourselves and those around us in an enhanced way. It meant seeing children being more confident, making friends easily and performing well in an area they previously hated.

I have witnessed some incredible transformations in my work with young children. One nine year old boy had been on a trip around Australia with his parents. On returning to school, the boy was put in a class behind his previous class because he had missed so much school. This meant he was no longer with his friends and he saw himself as dumb and that no one liked him. He became really clingy to/with his parents and avoided participating in sport or anything social with other children. We spent time using energy cleansing and visualization techniques so that he saw himself as confident and loveable. At the end of the year he very proudly came to show me his class Dux certificate. We used a special tape I had made for children often in the early days of our working together and this really cemented the new visions he made for himself.

Many children and teenagers have the worst possible vision of themselves. "I am dumb, fat, and useless, no one likes me, I am ugly and no-one cares." Some of these children come from very loving families yet the inner critic, or the ego voice, runs an inner dialogue that criticises; it reinforces negative messages we have heard in our childhood. With deep relaxation, particularly with positive visualization, this critical voice can be quietened so that the unconscious and conscious minds can hear some of the positive messages that reassure young people.

Now more than ever our children need reassurance and love through kindness and tenderness. The reassurance that comes from creative visualization goes deep within the psyche because it is being heard without filtering by the ego. Our children need to be reminded that they have a potential for goodness and greatness, no matter what has happened or they have done so far. The human spirit within our children needs more nurturing than ever before. The creation of positive images of themselves does direct children to believe they are capable and acceptable as they are. Those who perform best have positive mental images that they will achieve well. They often have families that support this by practising encouragement and praise and who focus on the positives in their lives rather than their shortcomings. Now we could bring this practice into schools to help those children whose families are unaware of the importance of this in the well being of their children.

> *"I'd prefer to see parents spending time with their children learning to visualize, rather than spending time in front of the television set or reading bedtime stories. It's important to teach yourself and your children manifestation techniques with visualization."*

Doreen Virtue, *The Care and Feeding of Indigo Children*

I have already mentioned that in 1998 I was given a small class of low achievers in English. They were all boys. I decided to work at changing both their mental and emotional perceptions of English classes and their inner beliefs and perceptions about how well they would perform at the end of term. We created 'the Best Report Ever' visualization. It involved taking the students into a quiet relaxed place and imagining taking home their very best report ever – how Mum reacts, how Dad reacts and how proud they feel within themselves. The students enjoyed the activity as they were able to feel positive about themselves and the body followed the mind. What they didn't realise was that their inner perceptions of their potential also changed. Every one of those boys took home the best report they had ever achieved! They were further surprised because they improved in all their subjects and not just English.

Dr Gerald Jampolsky the Director of the Centre for Attitudinal Learning in the US created an Accelerated Learning Technique for remedial readers at the elementary level. (See Appendix 1) A group of remedial readers used the tape at home every night for a three month period and at the end of the time they were re-tested and they had all increased their reading ages, some by as much as four years! The best news was this was achieved without extra tuition or extra work. I have created a visualization similar to Gerald's on the School Mastery CD 1 called "I Can Read Easily". The teachers using this CD have noticed instant changes in attitude towards reading and of course as students moderate all learning through their emotions this is the first step to changing performance. At last a tool for parents to use at home that the child will enjoy!

In NLP, thoughts are believed to direct the language one uses and both influence behaviour. If we can remind students to imagine and consider verbally the highest possible outcome or vision for themselves then we really give them the best opportunity to achieve positive results. It must be always linked to a high emotionally pleasant state. The repetition that is built into visualizations on tapes or CD's is very important for building new belief systems in the unconscious mind.

Real worriers and people with depression have a tendency to frighten themselves with their own negative patterns of thought, especially about the future. They rehearse the worst case scenario and the 'what if I fail?', 'I am not good enough' thought patterning and virtually talk themselves into despair and hopelessness.

Creative imagining with the most favourable outcomes is considered an essential activity for fast tracking personal achievements in all

areas of life. I firmly believe that with more awareness of the power of inner thought patterns, visualization and language, especially for children before ten years of age, we can help turn around the frightening escalation of failure and low achievement. We can give our children the tools for life that allow them to manage their negative feelings states and their emotionally destructive patterns BEFORE they get to puberty when everything accelerates and becomes even more unpredictable. The inclusion of creative visualizations into programs created by psychologists for school children like in the very successful "Friends" program validates the importance of the practice.

Managing stress, uncertainty and fear are the key areas in building a real resilience, for everyone. These emotional competencies are so important. The chances of a child becoming a serious abuser of drugs and alcohol, suffering mental illness, dropping out of school or becoming a suicide victim is intimately linked with their ability to love and accept themselves, and to be able to form deep connections with families and friends. The perception of lack of love is often at the core of a troubled child or teenager. This feeling is further complicated by their coping strategies or the absence of effective ones. Without healthy coping strategies many young people resort to acting out, withdrawing or drowning their emotional pain in some way. Teaching children the positive power of a healthy imagination can help all children.

Many parents and teachers have unknowingly become dream stealers. We have used the consciousness of the education system to unwittingly teach our children that, without school success, they will have little chance of life success. We need to change this. Indeed, I have worked with so many adults who held themselves back from promotions and better jobs because of the mental and emotional negative damage done at school, much of it unintentionally.

Let us see our young children and teenagers as having a 'call to greatness' that is different in all. We need artists, chefs, beauticians, roads workers as well as brain surgeons, teachers and engineers. Everyone is important in the fabric of our society. **Our capacity to make the world better in some way is really what we are all here for.** This is what we need to remind our children. All our children can do that, even those who never learn to read, who fall out of the school system or lose themselves to the drug culture, who ride motor bikes and have lots of tattoos or even those who spend time in prison. It is not about what job, where you live, or what has happened in the past, everyone can, starting today, do something that makes the world a better place.

I sometimes use the following small reading at funeral services, ponder on its words:

That a man is a success
Is one Who has lived well,
Laughed often and loved much;
Who has gained the respect
Of intelligent men
And the love of children;
Who has filled his niche
And accomplished his task;
Who leaves the world
Better than he found it
Who has never lacked appreciation
Of earth's beauty
Or failed to express it;
Who looked for the best in others
And who gave the best he had.

Adapted from Ralph Waldo Emerson:
That a Man is a Success

The power of imagination, of opening the possibilities of a better world and a better way of living, is within all of us. We keep ourselves from expanding this potential by being too busy, too absorbed in the external aspects of living, or by simply being unaware of this exciting possibility. We have the opportunity to teach our children well and to provide them with tools for becoming the very best they can be.

Nuts 'N 'Bolts

❖ Mental rehearsal and positive visualization does help build success strategies for children on all levels;

❖ Positive visualization can improve school achievement and emotional well being;

❖ Visualization can improve your ability to manifest your goals and intentions. It is important to teach children to imagine positive outcomes for themselves;

❖ Every child ever born is here to make the world a better place no matter who they are, what has happened in their lives or where they live;

❖ Visualization is a powerful tool that sports psychologists have been using for years;

❖ Visualization is a powerful life skill that helps improve emotional literacy and resilience;

❖ Visualization can help our children build their own dreams and to create the lives they really want to live. We all need dreams.

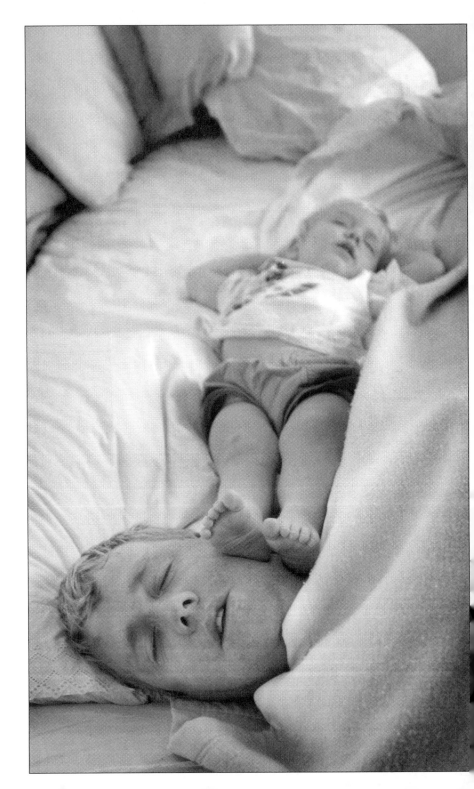

CHAPTER FIVE

real stress *and* emotional overload

*"Helping people better manage their upsetting
feelings – anger, anxiety, depression, pessimism
and loneliness – is a form of disease prevention.
Because the medical toll of distress is so broad,
relaxation techniques are being used clinically to ease the
symptoms of a wide variety of chronic illnesses."*

Daniel Goleman *Emotional Intelligence* p174-5 1996

Stress is a relatively modern word. It is a modern concept yet stress related illness is now estimated to account for around seventy five per cent of all illness.

Heart disease, high blood pressure, anxiety disorders, auto-immune disease, chronic fatigue and many mental illnesses are all believed to be affected by stress. We all know that the flight or fight response is naturally programmed into our bodies to help us act quickly in emergency situations. As the body and the mind have become overloaded with the fast pace of our modern life they often stay in this heightened state of tension, for long periods of time. This means that the normal body function of cell replacement, rest and renewal for revitalization, do not occur. The heightened level of cortisone in the body influences how we think, sleep and even how we digest our food unfortunately all negatively. We are asking for illness by living this way.

In my work I see people living under situations of emotional challenge. This affects the body in a very similar way to physical challenge, with weariness, insomnia, anxiety attacks and illness in its many forms. Long-term life crises such as school bullying, family conflict and bereavement are also evident physically.

What Creates Stress?

This is a list of issues that can cause stress especially for children and adolescents:

- ❖ Car accidents
- ❖ Bullying and harassment
- ❖ Nasty, malicious gossip
- ❖ Failing at school
- ❖ Depression
- ❖ Other mental illness
- ❖ Death of loved one
- ❖ Loss of job
- ❖ Abuse of any kind
- ❖ Teenage pregnancy
- ❖ Betrayal
- ❖ Criminal activity
- ❖ Alcohol or drug abuse
- ❖ Gender confusion
- ❖ Discrimination
- ❖ Serious illness
- ❖ Personal injury
- ❖ Family disharmony
- ❖ Sudden unexpected life change

Children display more signs of stress than ever before. The aggressive child, the hyperactive child, the miserable child and the sickly child are often displaying symptoms of stress. I believe our children are losing their childlike ways of being much earlier than before. **This is a disaster!**

I have also noticed that many anxious children with sleeping problems have been reacting to perceived fear rather than real fear. They have heard or watched something on the TV news and are imagining the same event happening to them or in their town or city. This also happens to sensitive children in classrooms with teachers who shout. They may never be yelled at as they behave well and yet the trauma to their energetic field is as if it is happening to them. This is how simple the causes of emotional overwhelm can be.

The apathy, lack of enthusiasm for living and the negativity expressed by children can be seen in some from as young as four. Healthy happy children have bright eyes, are quick to smile, have lots of energy and a deep connection to those closest to them. Life is fun and they have an amazing ability to bring adults into this same place. William Bloom in his wonderful book 'The Endorphin Effect' explains why children lose their benevolent connection to life:

> *"Children throb with a natural connection. But the slings and arrows of outrageous fortune start hitting early. Competitive siblings. Tough schools. Harsh media. Dangerous streets. Social injustice. All the noise of modern life. Hunger and pain. Each of these events, every childhood injury, physical and psychological, creates tension in the physical body.*
>
> *The result is that by the time most of us are teenagers we have lost that bubbling, continuous ability to feel life's natural beauty." p50*

Bloom goes on to describe how people lose their capacity to **feel** over time. They develop an armour that prevents their experiencing the endorphins of joy and bliss and the flow of benevolent energy.

An excellent way to get endorphins flowing back is by using the altered state that deep relaxation can bring. The need to create a sense of safety is important; people need to feel they are free of conflict and tension. I use a relaxed state in my counselling work because it feels so good! It also allows people, particularly children, to realise how it feels to be calm, safe and free from worry. The body in this state is open to insights and information accessed from a higher place within the personality. This is the inner guidance from our spirit instead of our ego-mask or our shadow.

(See Appendix 11 for Map of the Personality.) Intuition and 'gut feelings' are sourced from this place and when we search for answers from within ourselves we are less likely to be influenced by our ego voice, our shadow or what others want of us.

I recommend that you take the time to read Bloom's book. He explains, from both a scientific and spiritual perspective, how we can achieve happiness and joy, 'the bliss fields of life and living', without chemicals, drugs or alcohol. "The metaphysics of feel good" are found in the magic of silence and stillness and are especially important if we are unable to find them in daily life. You can find this magic easily in your life. Like me, Bloom does not want to give a temporary buzz or make you feel good for a short time, he wants to teach a practical strategy that is a positive in your life and builds your resilience and enjoyment of life.

We rarely live in the present moment. This is another reason why many of us, including our children, feel stressed. Our conscious mind spends so much time reliving our past, or frightening us with a possible future, that we create our own state of unease and tension. Yet it is so simple to find the real magic of stillness and silence. It does not require any course or study on a spiritual path, but simply making the time to stop, be still and become fully present in the moment.

Allowing our children to live lives where they are not time committed helps. Having spaces to day dream, to watch ants, to chat to your self and to be comfortable with your own company also helps. The modern parenting focus of getting children able to sing, dance, play music, play sport, know self defence and get extra tutoring so that they have lots of skills misses one key reality: **children need time to use their imagination in a fun and unstructured way.**

Another reason why children feel stress especially in education is that children are constantly reminded of doing well so they can have a good future; the importance of academic success is basically shoved down their throat from the minute they step into a school. When a child fails to meet satisfactory grades the sense of failing becomes ingrained in their sub conscious minds. As only around 30% of students get to university we need to replace this future focus on academic success to one that encourages learning for life and of mastering the present moment.

New presuppositions we may hold instead could be:

❖ That at any time people can become better educated;
❖ That being emotionally stable and happy is also an important aspect of life and learning;
❖ That not everyone is blessed in all multiple intelligences;
❖ That everyone has abilities and talents that will help them life an effective and valuable life;
❖ That we are all unique and different and that we learn differently;
❖ That school fails many of our children;
❖ That learning and growing RIGHT NOW in an environment that is safe and caring is what is important for our children.

The researchers who conducted the research of the emotionally illiterate boys who committed the school murders concluded that the lack of play activity contributed to the inability of these young men to be able to resolve their emotional problems with anything other than force. The use of play together with imagination helps children build strategies that mean they can resolve problems and have "emotional breaks" that can avoid conflict becoming violent and ultimately tragic.

Let me tell you about myself. I lived from a place of stress as a child as I was lost in amongst a large family. I had older brothers who enjoyed bullying and teasing me. My Mum was emotionally unavailable to me and was verbally toxic and abusive. I spent so much of my time trying to be noticed by her yearning for love, and the rest of the time I avoided her to avoid more emotional pain. My attention seeking behaviour was a desperate attempt to find love from her – if not her from anyone. At school I was tough and aggressive, a response to my powerlessness at home. I would also act as the class clown. None of these behaviours gave me what I wanted. They actually caused me more emotional pain and rejection. Physically I was a chronic nail biter and bed wetter, and I walked in my sleep. I had terrifying nightmares that were often repetitive, as I contemplated death as being a better option to living my life. All I remember from being raised as a country Catholic who attended church only a couple of times a year and had scripture classes at school was that I was definitely a sinner and that God punished sinners; more things for me to be frightened of in my confusing world. I can never remember being held, caressed or told I was loved.

I attempted suicide when I was seventeen years old when my sense of loneliness became too great. I remember feeling:

- ❖ Unloved;
- ❖ Misunderstood;
- ❖ Alone;
- ❖ Lost;
- ❖ Unheard;
- ❖ Disconnected from everything;
- ❖ Exhausted from pretending to be OK and happy;
- ❖ Frightened of living a life like this anymore;
- ❖ There was no-one to turn to physically, emotionally and spiritually.

The incident that triggered my suicide attempt was quite minor. I scored forty-five per cent in a politics essay in my first term at university. The sense of being a failure in the only area in my life I had any competence in was crushing. I had never failed an essay in my entire school life! All kinds of critical words I had ever heard from any adult or child experience in my life came rushing into my head. "You will never amount to anything!" "You are dumb, useless and stupid." "You will fail at University." "You think you are better than us......"

Fortunately my suicide attempt failed as I crushed some of the pills on my teeth and the taste was so awful I involuntarily vomited them back up.

In my counselling work I frequently find teenagers and adults who have contemplated or attempted suicide have the same feelings. Noticeably, I have attended many funerals where a person has suicided and yet NEVER has no-one attended. There have always been people present who obviously loved the person who took their own life. **The core problem leading to suicide seems to be** *the perception of a lack of love;* **the person had little self love and felt unloved and disconnected from others and our world.** Many parents are shattered when this concept is shared with them as they feel their love for their children was obvious.

Money, possessions and fine homes do not show love for a child. Rarely, in children's eyes, does cooking and doing their washing show them love; pushing and nagging about doing their homework, dressing cleanly and neatly certainly does not mean love. Nor does working long hours and being away on weekends. **Children perceive love from kindness, compassion, real acceptance and the presence of authentic safety and protection.**

Children and teenagers feel loved with you:

- ❖ Being there – having at least one parent around when they get home from school or on the weekend;
- ❖ Really listening, without judgement or criticism;
- ❖ Reminding them often that you love them, saying "I love you" while looking straight at them;
- ❖ Being kind and caring, rather than too disciplinarian;
- ❖ Connecting through touch, hugs, massages, or stroking;
- ❖ Safely sharing meals that are relaxed and full of open dialogue;
- ❖ Respecting their views and feelings even when you do not understand;
- ❖ Sharing activities they enjoy sharing with you – watching their videos, reading to them, watching clouds in the sky or the stars at night, going for picnics;
- ❖ Telling them real stories and happenings from your life that show when you failed or when you were successful;
- ❖ Appreciating their differences and avoiding comparing them with others;
- ❖ Lots of reassurance that they will be able to manage, work things out and enjoy life;

❖ Unexpected acts of kindness – buying their favourite ice cream, lollies, books or magazines to say thank you for doing chores, feeding the dog etc;

❖ Model life skills that build their own resilience to life – optimism, taking time out to unwind and rest, enjoying sports and hobbies; being community minded, respectful of other's rights and possessions;

❖ Going to watch them play sport, a musical instrument or dance – OFTEN;

❖ Taking lots of photos and displaying them around home;

❖ Creating magic moments that you repeat…like special family rituals around Birthdays, Christmas or significant rites of passage like leaving home, finishing school.

I have written of suicide in this chapter because many of the contributing factors that lead up to it are forms of emotional overwhelm that stem from feeling unloved and 'unspecial'. We underestimate the emotional confusion our children live through daily. Many cover it with a mask so that we think they are coping.

I have also observed in my counselling that overwhelmed teenagers are often "ungrounded." Essentially this means that an individual is energetically connected to the earth. While this may sound like something really fluffy and unimportant I know that ungroundedness and emotional overwhelm go together. When I am ungrounded I can get "scatty" with my thoughts and can feel anxious in my stomach. I also know that I give my best presentations when I am grounded and my best writing occurs from the same state.

There are simple techniques that can ground you:

1. Go for a walk and be aware of pounding your feet on the ground every now and again while taking deep breaths inwards.

2. Stand still and imagine your feet are glued to the floor or the ground. Then imagine roots or tentacles growing out from your feet down into the earth.

3. Imagine a ray of bright sunshine flowing down into your head right down your spine and then down into the earth. Then imagine that ray circles the core of the earth and returns back up into your body and back out through the top of your head.

4. Feel a bright ball of white light in your belly and imagine it is pulsing with energy and power.

5. Keep your knees off lock – slightly bended.

Remember being grounded can help you manage your emotional state, make better choices first with your thoughts and then with your actions. This is a life skill that we all need to master not just our children and teenagers. I have met just as many overwhelmed adults as I have of the younger generation.

So many times I have heard stories of terrifying things that are happening to children yet they have been unable to tell their parents. Children and teenagers so want to please their parents that they hide, at all costs, things that show they are not coping or are failing. Emotional honesty when done with gentleness and compassion can help free up emotional tension in our bodies. When we can share our emotional pain without fear of judgement or criticism we will share it more often. Have you ever come clean about a dishonesty or something you did that you wish you had not done? Once it is out and the truth spoken the body breathes a deep sigh of relief and the tension literally flows out of the body. This is one of the reasons why having someone to share our darkest secrets is so important and that counsellors and school chaplains or teachers who know how to listen, are worth their weight in gold. What completes this emotional honesty to its highest point is the act of forgiveness from the person who has been wronged. I have worked with adults who have harboured a regret for over thirty years because they worried about the other person's reaction. Quite often it has made them sick.

> *"Thinking stops when we are upset. But if we express feelings just enough, thinking re-starts…..One seriously flawed piece of handed-down 'wisdom' is the idea that when you start to cry you are out of control, falling apart, sick, going over the edge (whatever it is) and should do just about anything "to pull yourself together."*
>
> *Also outrageous is the list of things we are encouraged to do to "pull ourselves together." We are sent off to isolate ourselves and repress; we are encouraged to put alcohol into our lives, or pour caffeine into our hearts; we are given nicotine to fill our lungs, or icecream and cookies or ground cow muscle and deep fried potatoes to fill our guts. These are all supposed to be fine. Crying on the other hand – a genetically coded, wholly natural and intended means to rid the body of pain and toxicity is not supposed to be fine."*
>
> *Where did we go wrong?"*
>
> P74 *Time to Think* by Nancy Kline

We are meant to react to emotions as they occur in appropriate ways instead of repressing, hiding them, transferring them onto others or pretending we are managing them when we are obviously not. Nancy Kline's book is an insightful study of the importance of "listening" and its influence on our ability to think and to impact on other people's lives. Well worth a read. In a similar vein is Marshall B Rosenburg's book "Non Violent Communication." After reading these books I realised how poor most people are at authentic, caring, honest communication.

Emotional overwhelm is quite different to the normal swings of emotions that happen day to day. It is also important that our children and adolescents know that it is normal to feel up and down emotionally. As William Bloom says " Everyone has moods and cycles. That is just the way it is to be human and part of this universe." (*The Endorphin Effect*, 2001) The same importance needs to be placed on long term low energy and despair – it needs attending to as it could be clinical depression. Being moody and being mentally unwell are two quite different things.

The use of creative visualizations from a young age can help children put things into a more healthy perspective as well as allow them to relax and feel calm. The books by Maureen Garth (See resources at end of book) are wonderful for young children. They allow imagination to bring back the sense of safety and well being that William Bloom calls "the benevolent life force." (William Bloom, *The Endorphin Effect*, 2002) Teaching children to relax and to use their imagination can be incredibly healthy, leading to resiliency and protective factors that they take through life with them. It does help reduce stress and anxiety. It does help take them from the state of suffering and emotional pain, to one where they can feel calmer and with training they will be able to access this place, by choice, in moments of crisis throughout their lives. **The connection to our human spirit that is at the very core of who we are needs to be nurtured and encouraged.** That is where all our answers are, to every challenge and conflict that may arise in our lives. To reach this place of wisdom we need to still the inner critic, the voice of judgement within our minds and we need to be still and quiet so that we can hear this quiet voice of truth.

Nuts 'N' Bolts

Stress creates illness as well as mental confusion and emotional overwhelm

❖ Releasing natural endorphins is really important for health and well being on all levels;

❖ Imagination is essential for children to be able to build healthy emotional literacy and resilience in life;

❖ The perception of a lack of love for self and from parents is a key to emotional overwhelm and suicide;

❖ Show and tell and model children LOVE and COMPASSION;

❖ Teach children relaxation techniques by reading imaginary stories or by using relaxation products – they help the body relax, and self heal;

❖ Emotional well being is enhanced by being grounded in your body;

❖ Emotional honesty and forgiveness are powerful tools in healing our emotional stress and overwhelm.

energy *and* emotional states: teaching children how to be calm

*Relaxation is a skill that can be cultivated with practice.
It is not simply a feeling that stays in the mind; it ushers in
a host of body-wide physical changes that indicate a state of
low physiological arousal.*

Larry Dossey MD: *Healing Words*

Energy has become quite a catch word of the last ten years, especially in the area of personal wellbeing. So often, people complain of being tired or lethargic and wonder what is wrong with them. Our bodies are our own unique power houses and when we are eating well, keeping active and fit, and drinking plenty of water we are more likely to feel we have plenty of energy to get us through our daily living.

Statistics are frightening as to the number of overweight and obese children around the Western world today. Not only are children carrying excess body fat, they are probably feeling low in energy, which triggers emotions that keep them in an unhappy and negative emotional state. Overweight children are less likely to feel enthusiastic about their schooling, their friendships and life in general.

Healthy children have an enormous amount of energy and keep

'on the go' all day. Yet for some parents and teachers, the tired child is easier to manage.

As a mother of four highly energetic sons, I am fully aware of the challenge of parents to 'go the distance' with their children. My number three son was a great example of a highly spirited powerhouse of energy. He always awoke first for the day and was the last to go to sleep at night. I spent many, many hours trying to get him to bed at night, far beyond the time that his older brothers considered to be bedtime. I tried every negotiating endeavour known. Finally, when he was around four years of age, I decided he simply had too much energy to be ready for bed when everyone else was, including his parents. I gave him permission to put himself to bed when he was ready, giving clear directions on what was acceptable behaviour when the rest of us were asleep. And, I asked him to turn out the lights when he finally went to bed. No more fights and disagreements!

In the early days of the routine of putting himself to bed, I sometimes checked on my son and found him doing somersaults on his bed, playing 'matchie cars' on the floor, or building cubbies under his bed. The level of conflict in the family home reduced enormously when we allowed him to choose his own time for bed. This son is almost eighteen and still a late night owl; the only difference today is that he can now sleep in until late in the morning if he has created an appropriate uni timetable.

School can be a war zone for many children. There are so many things they have to be on guard for during the day that they tire themselves out. Verbal bullies cause them anxiety and concern; then there is the 'toxic teacher'; information overload; the challenge of the work and the terror of looking stupid in front of their peers. Constant pressure is a huge drain on children's energy fields. On top of that, a school day is often followed by other commitments like swimming training, music lessons and extra tutoring even though the child is still in a heightened state from being on guard all day. Finally, the home environment itself can also add to a child's anxiety level.

As we are all living energy centres a stress filled day will drain the energy available for other activities temporarily. Hyperactive children merely have a faster vibratory energy system than others. It is not a malicious intent. It just is. Expending excess energy is important for these children and the list on the following pages should help you to help your child manage their energy system. I am a high energy person and my husband is used to me baking late at night, or being really restless if I have been inside all day! I can be difficult to live with as I just keep going. Some nights I will be active for a couple of hours while everyone else is asleep.

Valerie Hunt in her fascinating book "Infinite Mind" describes many of her findings from her thirty year study at UCLA on the human energy field. This scientist discovered that electrical activity within the body is essential for life. She was also able to measure the energy centres of the body with special electromagnetic instruments and she was able to measure the vibratory patterns of the brain. Finally she was able to measure the energy of the aura or energy field outside the body. It is her research that showed that a person's energy field can be expanded by having a cold shower, a swim or by walking barefoot on grass. That is why by gently stroking a person's energy field about 15 centimetres from the body can create a sense of relaxation. When a person's electromagnetism reached a certain level "there was evidence of improved motor performance, emotional well being, excitement and advanced states of consciousness." (Valerie Hunt, *Infinite Mind*, 1996, p32)

This means that it is time for us to be mindful of human energy and how it can be expanded or calmed depending on the current state of the individual's energy state.

I believe that children regain their energy in a number of ways:

1. Firstly, children need to be able to switch off from paying attention, both to others and to their environment. This allows them time and opportunity to follow their own instincts to renew their energies. Some will spend time alone, sometimes talking to themselves in a fantasy-like activity. In this way, they drop the heightened protective guard they have held all day. Time to be alone is especially important for the more introverted child as they tend to feel safest when they are by themselves;

2. Some children need to play physically and often in an unstructured way like chasing the dog in the yard or kicking a ball around. As they unwind and drop their defensive states, their imaginations are released. Physical activity also helps them to disperse excess energy from feeling frustrated or even frightened at school or in the home;

3. Some children need to feel nourished by loved ones, with hugs and outward signs of emotional connectedness. Then they let their guard down. Often extroverted children like to chat about their day with someone older as this helps them to 'debrief' and 'recharge their batteries'.

It is important to be mindful of transition times for children so that they can find their own ways of re-energising when they come home from school or somewhere else. Pauses in the process of constant educational learning and physical development are so important because the gaps give time for their imaginations to kick in.

Children's inner world helps them to diffuse stress. Some children take to using my visualization techniques on days when they feel really wound up; these work within ten minutes. The children take them to their rooms and they really de-stress, and may have a nap too, so that they are able to reconnect to a relaxed alert state before they begin their after-school activities. My sons usually ate heartily after school. They had a drink, usually water or milk (never cordial or fruit juice), and then bolted for the outside door. Sometimes they 'chilled out' in front of the TV for half an hour before heading outside.

Tips for Calming Hyperactive Children

Hyperactive children can be particularly challenging. I have some tips for concerned parents and teachers. But first, know that there will be times when nothing you do will make much difference. When you realise that this is such a time, make yourself a cup of tea or coffee, shut yourself in your bedroom and play some relaxing music. Take a Tim Tam if there are any left! Or you go for a walk! Then, remember good moments in your child's life and think positive and calming thoughts of love about them. Send him or her a rainbow of love and breathe deeply.

Important ways you can make a difference with your child's behaviour are:
1. Keep your child away from cool drink, cordial, fruit juices and anything with colouring, preservatives and added sugar. Maybe visit a nutritionalist, naturopath or homeopath to get help with understanding the huge influence diet has on behaviour;
2. Have your child checked out by a chiropractor who specialises in children, to ensure that their spinal and cranial plates are balanced;
3. Honestly check your own stress levels. Children are often emotional barometers for one, or both, of their parents;
4. Encourage as much free unstructured outside play as possible. This may mean many trips to the park but being outside in nature helps. Try it, you may realise that your child is much harder to manage when kept inside for too long. That's why after school can be tricky if you work!

5. Learn how to give back and foot massages. Better still, learn how to give reiki or therapeutic touch and offer it to your hyper active child;

6. Many children do not know HOW to calm down or even what calm feels like. Teach them relaxation and calmness at as early an age as possible. Read to them lots, try using relaxation products at night before sleep time and teach them to breathe deeply and how to be grounded;

7. Teach them to be comfortable with silence, if not stillness! That means having a home where silence is familiar – no sounds.

8. Bathing or swimming always helps; it calms unsettled babies;

9. Try aromatherapy; the brain responds to the calming effect of many smells – lavender, sandalwood & jasmine. There are some excellent combination essences for calming;

10. Reassure your child that even though they are highly spirited and cannot pay attention for long you always love them. Help them to tune into what they are feeling under their hyperactivity. What is it they feel? Do they feel angry; hurt; unloved; dumb; or naughty? Use life enhancing language.

11. Surround them with calming music from classical to nature ones. They help change the water inside the body (70% of us is water) by changing the molecular structure according to the sounds of the music.

12. Give your child lots of opportunities to be creative – with drawing and painting, music, building or creative play. Allow them to become absorbed in the act of creation – this helps release emotional energy as he or she discovers the wonders and fun of creativity!

13. Teach the 'cook's hook up', a technique from Paul Dennison in his educational kinesiology program (Appendix 10)

14. Really listen and be present with your child, at least once a day. Many hyperactive children question authority and react negatively to manipulation or inappropriate use of power. They are often very sensitive and spiritually aware underneath their mask of confidence and nonchalance so never lie to them or make up an answer. Be honest because they will know;

15. Try calming bush flower essences. These are made by Ian White, a third generation Australian naturopath, are inexpensive and can be very effective (See Appenix 12);

16. Finally, be very mindful of your thoughts. Hyperactive children pick up negative thoughts very quickly and react and respond

to them. Change negative words to words that are encouraging and positive. Read 'Raising Your Spirited Child' by (Mary Sheedy Kurcinka);

17. Hold the highest vision for your child. See him or her loved, accepted and valued just as they are;

18. Some children are capable of learning faster than the teaching profession can imagine. They may be our inventors, change agents, computer programmers and leaders of tomorrow as they have so much energy, original vision and drive;

19. Consider the effect of birth order on your child – read Michael Grose's book "Why First Borns Rule The World And Last Borns Want To Change It";

20. If managed well in childhood, hyperactive children can mature into very capable focussed adults who are energetic, optimistic and resilient. On the other hand, being overwhelmed by a label of being difficult and nonconformist may cause them to struggle with the challenges of managing their lives as they grow older. Maintain firm boundaries, negotiate and be kind.

21. Turn it around, learn from your hyperactive child the gifts of honesty, perseverance, patience and creative problem solving;

22. If 'all of the above' fails, do some serious 'personal growth work' to improve your ability to cope with ANYTHING! Many hyperactive and 'in your face' children are here to accelerate their parents' personal healing journeys. Remember also, some of your child's behaviours are linked to generational patterns that could do with some healing.

Refilling Energetically

We are all made up of energy and have our own electrical fields and vibrations. Other people have their energy vibrations and some may be more compatible to us than others. Energy exchanges 'happen' between people all the time. Stop and feel it the next time you meet or talk to someone. Feel how drained you feel after spending time with someone in emotional crisis or depression.

It is important to learn how to fill our own tanks of energy without having to take from others. Natural energy from nature is freely available to us. Feel how energised you feel after a swim in the ocean! The same happens after a walk in the fresh air – even better at the beach or in the bush away from traffic. In the same way, the sooner we teach our children how to manage their own energy fields the easier it will be to live with them, these little cherubs who are labelled with all sorts of names. The highly spirited are very unique individuals who have come here with their own life mission too!

Calmness and deep relaxation are ways to refill our energy tanks. They allow our minds to find clarity in a rapidly changing world. Have you been calm and relaxed today? Remember that sometimes children resonate at a significant adults energy system rather than their own. So get yourself a copy of Paul Wilson's **Instant Calm** and master some of the calming exercises or activities that he explains. They really do work!

Nuts 'N' Bolts

❖ Childhood obesity is linked to inactivity in childhood;

❖ Stress can drain children's energy fields;

❖ Too much organised activity can make children tired – they have no time to fill their energy tanks;

❖ Hyperactive children are challenging to parents and teachers – there are many non-chemical ways of managing them;

❖ Allow children to have gaps in their lives to choose their own ways to entertain or amuse themselves;

❖ Everyone benefits from calmness, stillness and SILENCE. These are learned states useful for those who live life 'to the full' in high energy states;

❖ We are merely energy systems with varying degrees of vibration happening;

❖ There are many ways to quieten our hyperactive children – keep trying;

❖ Safe calm environments create calmer children;

❖ The imagination is very important to keep encouraging in children for as long as possible;

❖ Knowing how to fill and re-channel energy cups is really important with children;

❖ Use calming techniques on yourself.

transcendence *and* adolescence

I have found that relaxation exercises which include attending to breath and muscle relaxation can help students to become alert and focused, as well as foster a more harmonious learning environment. I have also worked with visualization or guided imagery and see the benefits for many children of awakening the imagination, satisfying curiosity about "altered states of consciousness" in healthy ways and gaining new insights about their goals and gifts"

Rachael Kessler: *The Soul of Education,* p131, 2000

The journey from childhood to adulthood is bumpy, confusing and frightening. There are many changes happening on all levels – mind, body and spirit. Statistics show that, today, we have more teenagers struggling from mental illness, poverty, homelessness, violence, teenage pregnancy, crime and alcohol and drug abuse.

Drug use and abuse has increased considerably over the last ten years. Frighteningly so! I question experts about what is behind this increase.

The usual answers are:

- ❖ It is normal teenage experimentation;
- ❖ Drugs are now much more available and accessible to young people;
- ❖ There are more emotional challenges for today's teenagers;
- ❖ It is a way to avoid pain, usually emotional;
- ❖ Peer pressure – driven by the desire to belong;
- ❖ It is a way to de-stress and relax;
- ❖ Legal drugs, including tobacco, alcohol and pharmaceutical drugs have increased in use and social acceptance;
- ❖ Teenagers are looking for peak experiences and find drugs a great way to have them;
- ❖ It is a way to escape unhappiness and loneliness;
- ❖ It builds a false sense of confidence and wellbeing.

In April 2000, I lost a niece, Susan, to an accidental overdose of heroin. My sister lost a beautiful though troubled daughter. Susan did not hang out with 'unemployed, teenagers from broken homes' but was caught up in the drug scene that led to her heroin addiction through her work in a Perth law firm. Here was a world where money was abundant, as were stress and power games, all woven into an unhealthy blend. It created a need for a quick easy way to escape the pressure and to feel confidently exalted, high on life.

When my niece moved to Melbourne, she spiralled into eight years of hopeless heroin addiction. She 'de-toxed' many times and went on an eighteen month long methadone program, but unfortunately she developed a bi-polar disorder. The overload on her system of medications for this mental illness and her continued occasional use of heroin were too much for her, and she died in her thirty third year of life.

Susan told me of how the powerful seduction of heroin rarely left her mind, or her body, from the time she became addicted. This was no matter how hard she tried; she had a love-hate relationship with heroin. The high that she described when heroin flowed into her veins, however, was something that many of us find naturally in our lives. It is the expanded and euphoric feeling I experience after a deep meditation, a nurturing massage, or a gentle reiki experience.

Through Susan, the way was opened for me to consider the need to give our children and teenagers the opportunity to experience moments of heightened pleasure and wellbeing without drugs of any kind. The need for transcendence is part of every human being's journey to awareness and maturity.

There are many ways parents and teachers can help find this heightened sense.

The Athletic High

In Australia we are 'pretty sporting mad'. Many visitors who were in Sydney for the 2000 Olympic Games were amazed at the passion we express for sport in any shape or form.

I feel sure that we are so enthusiastic because sport elevates us to a pleasurable state that we enjoy. This state can be experienced without alcohol and drugs.

I find that when I watch the Olympic on television, I experience many feelings. I have ended up in tears of joy and sadness, found myself cheering and yelling aloud, and I have felt choked up with pride and a strong sense of patriotic fever when an Australian wins an exciting race or match. When an underdog, from anywhere in the world, overcomes incredible difficulties just to compete – remember the unheard of swimmer who swam in front of thousands of spectators for his tiny country and was hopelessly outclassed. His guts at competing and completing the course won hearts and a sense of euphoria followed. It was a great example of the potential power of sport to reach a place of heightened emotions. Not just the winners experience these feelings!

I am a 'seldom TV watcher' and so have limited exposure to the many magic moments in sporting history. Sport has huge potential in a healthy development of the reality of drug-free highs. It is particularly important for boys to be able to enjoy physical activities and sport to this degree. Schools and communities can help by being as supportive as possible in the continued development of sport and athletic pursuits. It is a drug prevention tool.

I draw attention to the work of Gayelene Clews, an Olympic Sports Psychologist. She promotes the same directive, that sport can build life and social skills and is really important for our developing youth, especially men. 'The Games We Play' is a program that Gayelene brings to schools and it is an important way to build self esteem as well as health and a sense of wellbeing. Elite sports people have positive messages to bring to our teenagers, messages that build resilience to life's knocks and hope for becoming the best they can be. Sport also brings opportunities to build connectedness between children and teenagers, and this is an important attribute of healthy teenage development. Plus sport and active play encourages physical activity and that helps burn up kilojoules and build up energy, both incredibly important today with our soaring obesity statistics.

Outdoor Pursuits

I again mention the importance of families encouraging the growth of a healthy relationship with Nature, the 'Outside World'. Being a farmer's daughter, I had a childhood where I was able to fully embrace the natural world. I felt its potential to be a place of comfort and enlightenment. 'Country kids' are often more aware of the passing seasons, the importance of working with Mother Nature and of the cycle of birth, life and death. As children, my siblings and I were helping to deliver lambs and pups by the age of six. It was very exciting to help bring a lamb into the world. Birth is a very transcendent experience – a natural high.

Some of my experiences also built my sense of responsibility as we were part of the workforce on our farm. We helped shift mobs of sheep and feed the animals. As soon as our feet could reach the pedals we were taught to drive so that we could help check on stock or take Dad's lunch out to him in the paddocks. My first year at university in the city was a major culture shock for me. There was too much noise, traffic and 'rushiness'! I understand how the alienation of city life can contribute to addictive behaviour, depressive thoughts or a sense of disconnection from people and things that matter.

The importance of pursuits outside the four walls of home and the classroom has been known for a long time. The creator of 'Outward Bound', a national adventure organization, identified the transformational powers of life in nature back in the post war years. He created opportunities for experiences that removed people from the comfort zones of familiar environments and developed challenges that really stretched them. There is still room for schools to focus on at least one major physical challenge as part of the upper school program, made readily available to both tertiary and non-tertiary bound students.

Adventures on the tall ship the 'Leeuwin' are a great example of physical challenge. Being part of a team that is responsible for the safety of everyone on board the ship is certainly character building. The challenge of scaling the masts to set the sails is one of the special tests of personal courage available while onboard ship. Close supervision is provided, by people with expertise and a passion to help young people grow and develop, and allows this experience. It is an excellent form of character building as well as a positive way to experience drug-free highs just as school camps can be.

Many years ago, I was the only female staff member on a canoe trip for eighteen upper school students. We were in the South West corner of Western Australia and everything was fine for the first four days as we paddled up the beautiful Frankland River. In the evenings we trekked and found a place to camp. On the fifth day, we paddled back down the Frankland River and were to cross the Walpole estuary to make our way up the Deep River. Half way across the estuary, a strong storm blew up and two of the canoes headed out towards the ocean. The strong winds and rain made it quite scary for all of us but the other canoes were able to beach at the opening of the Deep. The male staff members headed off to rescue the two canoes that were in trouble. We set to work to find wood and get a fire going; it was now quite dark as we put up the rain drenched tents. Finally, the missing crews and their rescuers returned amidst an ecstatic welcome. The atmosphere of the camp changed from that point on as the frightening experience had bonded the group. That night much of the gear was wet and so everyone piled into the bigger tents, where we shared whatever dry sleeping gear there was. Staff and students bundled in together. The final night of this camp took place under an amazingly starry sky. It was a wonderful evening of singing, joke telling and dreaming of the first good meal we would have once we returned from the wilderness.

The transformation that occurred during the six days of that camp was unbelievable. We were all able to experience a **'high on life'** feeling that many young people are seeking through drugs. Even just recalling the last night of that camp makes my heart feel expanded.

My sons are all keen surfers. The ocean has provided them with some of their finest and worst moments over their last ten years. It will probably continue to do so for many years to come. There is something very special about the ocean and the soul of those who choose and love to be part of it. Encourage your children or your students to find this connection and to nurture it.

The following piece was written in 1998 by a boy in a Year 12 English class. It captures beautifully the potential of a connection with the ocean:

Mark's Story

The boy – no, he's a young man now – the young man stands outside the house in the crisp, clear, early morning autumn air. The arrow of the weather vane stays firmly embedded in a Northern direction even though there is scarcely a breeze to move it. The sound of waves breaking on sand is audible even though the beach is a far way away. So the man gets into his car and drives to paradise.

When the man crests the sand dune separating the beach from the rest of the world he is confronted by the sight of big glossy blue tubes reeling and spitting all the way up and down the beach. They are perfect crystal giants, their lips parting the troughs and kissing the sand with a crack like a rifle. They spend their short lives wandering the oceans until they reach shores far from their origin, never to return to their mindless treks. They, like most natural things on this earth, have the capacity to bring joy and beauty to people who know how to utilize them, those who have the ability to ride the sometimes wafer-thin edge between pleasure and pain and death with equal assurance. This, they bring to those who don't know how to ride them, or why, those people who are ignorant of the beautiful, timeless gifts that they bring.

He is the only person on the beach. Today his experiences will not be shared by any other man or woman or child hunting their own perfection. He jumps out over the small white froth churning at the edge of the shore and is shocked by the coldness of the water; it shocks him into full awareness. He paddles out through the channel and looks into the gaping mouths of the hollow, grinding, spitting barrels as they rise up over the sand bank, screaming a challenge to the young man, "Ride us! Ride us! Take the risk and reap the reward!" He paddles over, parallel to the shoreline, until he sits right on the peak. His first three waves are taken to ease him into the rhythm of the ocean, to give him a feel of the potential power gathered in the water around him. It is a lot bigger than it looked from the beach.

When he paddles back out, the man sits up on his board and looks out to the lumpy horizon. And he sees a huge set line heading straight for him. He lies back down and starts paddling for all his worth. As he floats over the wave in front of him he sees that the next wave is the bomb. It is huge; the biggest wave he has ever seen. But it is perfect, and seems to call to him, to ride it, to walk the tightrope over a bottomless pit, to risk his whole being for one short moment of bliss. The decision is not a hard one to make. He swings around and paddles into it.

All rational thought is pushed from his mind. He can no longer hear anything around him, and his body feels as if it is floating in space, weightless. It is one of those tubes where he doesn't need to fight against the wave to stay in there; what his mind is thinking is totally detached from what his body is doing. An angel picks him up and pushes him through the great, gaping, blue, swirling vortex of life. He is moving at the speed of light and at the same time is perfectly still. At this time, this infinitesimal particle of time in his whole existence, he realises that he has the power to do whatever he wants in his life, that he can change the lives of others, and that, when he is here, encased in water, a simple element abounding all over the planet, he is as close to God as he can get without having to die.

And suddenly his glimpse of heaven is gone, and he is pushed out into his own world again. He is almost regretful that the journey is over. And as he sits in the water, with salty tears of joy drenching him, screaming to the universe with uncurbed emotion, another man walks over the sand dune; not a surfer, but an old fisherman. He sees the waves, and he sees a man laughing and screaming and crying all at once, and he recalls a time when he could partake in the same act of worship, a time when he felt the same as this young, fit man.

"I know how you feel, son" he says quietly. "I know just how you feel."

Mark Jendrzejeczak, 1998

The 'buzz' and thrill that comes from the physical mastery of challenges like rock climbing, abseiling, high ropes courses and the like is a great way for teenagers to taste a place beyond the normal. It is a form of healthy risk taking. We all grow when we challenge our comfort zones, whether physical or emotional. The ocean seems to be especially helpful for teenage boys to nurture their desires to seek thrills, and it is good for their souls. It is sad that the threat of litigation has "tamed" down many school camps and expeditions as it will take away this type of transcendent experiences for our young.

Artistic and Musical Expression

The 'Arts' have been a source of wonder and awe for centuries. Great musicians and singers have stirred our hearts and drawn our spirits out to soar to elevated places for eons. It is no different now.

It is not, however, just the great talents of the world that can do this. At a musical eisteddfod you can feel the same awe and wonder at the giftedness of children and adults as they play or sing their way through their items. Similarly, at the Rock Eisteddfod where schools spend months creating unique school productions that involve both dance and a sense of theatre the amount of exalted energy present at the heats of these events is something to be experienced. Everyone wins, even if an individual school does not take home the award.

Children and teenagers taking part in school plays and musicals also experience a heightened feeling of 'being'. A dedicated talented teacher in one of our local primary schools puts on a school musical most years and the growth in confidence and the sheer exhilaration experienced by the students is amazing. To succeed to that point, there are many hours of preparation, rehearsal and a working together of the group for a shared goal. Incredibly important life skills are involved and the exalted high on performance nights is a great example of a drug-free lift.

Rachael Kessler in her excellent book the 'Soul of Education' talks of 'the urge for transcendence' that young people seek. She includes the following quote:

> *Adolescents of all ages need ecstatic experience to become adult, and if the culture will not provide it they will seek it in any case, often in ways which do them harm*

> *B. Neville*

Sometimes the 'urge for transcendence' translates into accidents, near death experiences, drugs that alter states of awareness, and alcohol abuse. Kessler explored the fascination of death in the young and identified that some suicides were not the result of despair and hopelessness but rather a "quest for a life-affirming experience of transcendence". This quest can be fed by poets, song writers and people of hero status who have died, like Michael Hutchence and Kurt Cobain.

In Kessler's book (p115-118), the term 'to transcend' means a variety of things:

- ❖ to be lost or immersed in a play, dance or creative process;
- ❖ "flashes of intensity" against a 'dull background' of ordinary days;
- ❖ to rise above, or pass beyond, a human limit;
- ❖ reaching beyond ordinary life and consciousness;
- ❖ opening to the domain of spirit.

We can all benefit by remembering how impressionable and naïve our teenagers are and prepare them as positively as possible to be discerning. It is important to continue to make room in our schools for the arts, for school performances and bands. This means also art for creative pursuits and for pleasure; creative writing, drawing and music to encourage individual expression in a non-assessable way.

Without these experiences teenagers may go looking for highs from somewhere else.

Deep Connectedness and the Power of Truth

In homes and classrooms that are safe, and where everyone is respected, there is an amazing potential to experience deep connectedness through the sharing of honest dialogue. I have experienced this many times in classrooms. Often what begins as a curriculum driven task has ended up as something very different. One such time was with a class of Year Eight students in a Catholic College. We began the lesson with a story from the religious education text, on the topic of what living like a Christian really meant. When I invited the students to share their experiences and ideas there was a gradual opening of truths among us. This created something very beautiful and powerful. These thirteen year olds spoke of losing loved ones and of their fears about the world. They then began to ask the questions that many young people do when trying to come to understand the concept of God:

❖ Why would God create a place like hell if he really loves us unconditionally?

❖ If we leave our bodies when we die, how are we supposed to recognise our loved ones when we get to the world beyond?

❖ Why does it feel so special or sacred to watch the sun rise on a beautiful morning when we are supposed to find God in Church?

❖ Why do people have a party after a funeral?

❖ How long does it take our souls to leave our bodies after we die?

I was staggered with the depth of the questions these young teenagers expressed.

It showed me clearly that they were searching for answers to the meaning and purpose of life just as Rachael Kessler expresses in her seven gateways of the soul of education. (see Appendix 6) They involved topics considered to be part of the Year Twelve curriculum. That day showed me, very clearly, that teenagers start questioning the deeper questions of life early and they need an opportunity to explore these issues in a safe environment. The connectedness that we all felt during this time of open dialogue was profound and the class went through the recess break without anyone wanting to move.

In my work I meet many spiritually aware and wise young people, from six years of age upwards, who have an amazing understanding of the meaning of life. Many of these young people are struggling to live in families that are completely unaware, following the pursuit of money and power, expressing a lack of caring of others and a narrow view of the world. Aware and wise young people are often global in the way they see the world so that peace and environmental preservation are very important to them. I call them 'old souls', for the want of a better term, yet they really struggle in our school systems. Sadly, they often ease disillusionment by drug and alcohol abuse. These sensitive ones suffer deeply from a lack of love and concern for others that is about them. Unless they can find healthy outlets for their ideas and feelings through involvement in the arts, sports, or the presence of a significant, caring adult, then they are at high risk in life, particularly in their early adult years. Some of these people find great comfort in a religion or through spiritual practices like meditation, chanting and prayer. Some seek answers through pursuing occult and cult groups.

Nurturing the Inner World

We all have an inner and an outer world. Both are with us at all times in some form or another. There are many terms and words used to describe what is meant by our 'inner world', and these can be misleading. Simply put, we all have the ability to shift our focus of attention from what is happening outside of us to what's happening inside. We can change our connection with what is around us with our intent, as when we daydream, and we create an 'altered state' from our normal waking way of behaviour.

I believe firmly that we need to bring 'relaxation' and silent time to think into our lives. This time allows answers to come into our minds and creative imagination opportunities into our days, and into our classrooms. It is best from an early age and followed through to the final years of schooling, and beyond. Besides being an excellent way to teach effective stress management for later life, I believe that relaxation and silent time nurtures healthy development of an inner world where children and teenagers can alter their own states of awareness, without needing drugs or alcohol.

The human imagination is a greatly under utilised aspect of the human mind. With new understanding of how the brain REALLY works, we are able to take some simple principles into our classrooms. Andrew Fuller, a well-known Australian expert on 'resilience', has a special interest in teenagers. He wrote the following:

> *In a world where people rush faster and faster, work longer and longer, and laugh less and less, it is important to remember that it is our connections to other people that give meaning to our lives. It is worth reminding ourselves of the four questions asked in many forms of traditional healing.*
>
> *When did you stop singing?*
> *When did you stop dancing?*
> *When did you stop listening and telling stories?*
> *When did you become disenchanted with the sacred place of silence?*

Andrew Fuller: From Thriving to Surviving (1998)

Disenchanted, alienated teenagers have lost all those aspects of the human spirit. Schools place less and less importance on singing, dancing, listening to and telling stories, and silence in the pursuit of academic excellence. Many families and communities also place less and less value on them. I believe passionately in the importance of these 'soul' aspects for the healthy growth and development of our X future generations. I remember a sixteen year male student telling me, after a session to help him heal deep grief over losing his mother to cancer, that the deep relaxation and connection to his inner self that he was feeling from the session was better than two cones of marijuana. He also felt he hadn't really lost all of his mother because in the imaginary world he felt he connected to her again.

Inside Every Child is a Potential for Greatness

Unfortunately we seldom tell our children this. Yet they need to hear it, many times, especially throughout their formative years.

While our school system continue to hand out accolades only to the academically brilliant and sporting champions we are telling the rest of our students that they are a failure. So many students leave school with a deep sense of being inadequate. This may be at a deeper level than we can ever imagine. I have discovered this from the stories I hear in my consulting room. Alcohol and drugs used to numb the pain from this sense of inadequacy only make it worse. I wish we could prevent all teenagers from smoking and using marijuana until they are well into their twenties, at least. I find that regular use of drugs in the early teens reduces motivation for life, creates a higher incidence of depression or negative emotional states, and slows reaction time when driving or working machinery. Marijuana dulls the brain's ability to manage complex tasks and undertake decision making, and these are two key features of a teenager's formative years. The decisions many regular marijuana users make about their schooling and their relationships are seldom based on hope and optimism for attaining the highest vision for the future.

Deep Relaxation

Teenage years are a time when our fledgling adults are spreading their wings and sampling life in its many forms and fashions. Teenagers often live with a strong inner critic and the voice of judgement within their heads as they compare themselves to others and life's expectations of them. Being able to reach a deep place of inner calmness and stillness can help them feel better about themselves. Deep relaxation quietens the inner voices. Very deep relaxation combined with deep breathing can create an altered state of awareness that feels 'out of the ordinary'.

Deep relaxation is a cheap, gentle form of transcending the normal mundane life of study, school and complex relationships. If you could see the faces of a whole classroom of students or a room of teenagers AFTER a twenty minute of guided relaxation you would know it is the truth.

The funny thing about relaxation in the classroom is that it also usually helps students become more alert and to concentrate on their tasks. A more positive calmer learning environment is created. Using breath and muscle relaxation exercises brings more oxygen into the body and that is important for the whole body, not just the lungs and circulatory system.

Teachers need to be very mindful of a possible negative reaction to the terms meditation and guided visualization. Fundamentalist Christian groups believe the practice to be blasphemous, especially when there is any reference to inner wisdom and guidance, because they believe all guidance comes from God. Teachers need to keep their own religious and spiritual beliefs well away from the classroom. Other negative reactions could come from the activity being considered a 'New Age practice'. Be mindful of these reactions yet do not let them stop you from bringing the benefits of relaxation and visualization to as many students as possible. There are many imagination exercises that are perfectly safe for classrooms to use.

They can enhance students' learning as well as bring 'the magic of silence' into the classroom.

In primary school it is important to keep the exercises brief and to allow children to draw or play for a short time after a relaxation or visualization activity. Be prepared for students to choose to read silently rather than participate, if they prefer. Sometimes, especially after an active lunch break, a relaxation activity may end up as a short nap for a child. I think this is incredibly valuable and beneficial for the child as they may be able to focus better on their work afterwards. I believe very strongly in teaching stretching and effective waking up skills following a relaxation activity. These same skills can work when students feel tired or sleepy in general and not just after a relaxation session.

For older students who have longer attention spans and who are more aware of their inner worlds, guided relaxations for longer periods of time are possible. I find that activities that include high self esteem messages like: "you are enough no matter what", or, "who you are is valuable and worthwhile', are particularly useful in building positive beliefs in our teenagers. **Students who use these guided relaxations weekly say they manage stress much better, and that they feel more stable.** I firmly believe guided relaxation is a way of strengthening our higher self and of disempowering the negative inner critic. This helps everyone, not just the teenagers.

Other benefits from silence are insight, renewal and discovery. Emotional intelligence is helped greatly by 'the magic of silence' as a place where emotions can be explored and solutions found: "Periods of silence not only soothe the soul but allow the associations, consolidation and imprinting needed for effective learning" (Kessler: p52, 2000). Insight, renewal and discovery can help an older child or teenager to get a better sense of themselves and this growth of self awareness is important.

In the classroom, opportunities to reflect on self and on the stories of others are very helpful in expanding a vision of how things are, and how they can be. This practice brings with it the teacher's responsibility to protect a student's solitude if they choose to keep their thoughts and feelings to themselves. Confidentiality must be respected at all times. This is an incredibly valuable practice for teenagers to understand. So much personal pain is caused in schools from gossip mongers.

For secondary students, I firmly believe in the importance of a retreat which is a planned excursion into nature to allow students to participate in activities that build emotional bondedness and reflection as students prepare for a new step in their lives.

Many youth camps are retreats. A group retreat that encourages students to open to their inner worlds is a powerful tool for growth and development. A chance is given to spend time alone in nature, with no tasks to complete, and this time can be very revealing. Many students find they remember these retreats for the rest of their lives as they were a time when they felt fully aware of themselves and in touch with a place of inner strength. These moments are so helpful in the development of a strong sense of identity, which adolescents are searching for.

> *"Sit down, spend some quality time with yourself, and discover **what is truly important to you**. Find it. Hold on to it. Live it. No matter how hard it may be, keep a positive attitude. Be happy within yourself and what you have right now, every single day. Find that solace within yourself, for anything else can only make things better."*

These words of wisdom come from Dave Pelzer in his book " Help Yourself". This man 's story of survival through his three books "A Child Called It", " The Lost Boy" and "A Man Called Dave" was simply the most inspiring and challenging life story I have ever read. His ability to find comfort within himself was one of his key resiliency protective factors that enabled him to survive his hideous, violent childhood.

The importance of the concept "retreat" is that it allows you to step back from your normal life to see things differently. Retreats work best when they are set in nature and have supportive, aware teachers to lead them. Combined with a rite of passage, like the end of school, they can become life changing experiences as they mark the closure of one part of their life and celebration of a major life change.

Teachers and parents can model the practice of silence in a positive healthy way for their teenagers. Modelling allows children and teenagers to see silence as something positive. It can be seen as a powerful tool to manage the stresses of our busy, rushed world, and it is greatly underestimated. There is something quite magical when people sit comfortably in silence, becoming human beings rather than 'human doings'. This is the natural way to give a sense of relaxation and inner calmness, without drugs like marijuana.

Our teenagers are living in a very different world to the one we grew up in. I firmly believe that now they need their parents during adolescence more than ever before. Drug affected or addicted teenagers can come from any family, any cultural group and any community. I have some very special friends who are loving caring parents and yet who have a daughter who struggled with a heroin addiction. **Don't be complacent or judgemental; be well informed, involved with your kids and especially be vigilant.**

I personally believe the increasing drug problem has a lot to do with the twentieth century pursuit of materialism. Money and material wealth are valued more than a family within a caring community. In this twenty first century we can ALL take a long hard look at our world and our relationships. We can make some significant changes so that our children grow up feeling safe, loved, supported and protected from a horrible reality. All teenagers have issues of self value at some time or another. As they are also aware of the availability of drugs that can alter feeling states rapidly and take away pain, they are easy targets for drug use. 'Anna's Story' by Bronwyn Donaghy is a good book to have in your home, to read and to talk about. It tells of Anna Woods who died at fifteen after taking an ecstasy tablet. Her family have devoted time and energy to making sure no other lives are lost in this tragic way.

Family awareness and open communication about the potential for harm with illicit drugs is essential in the drive/war against drugs. The Federal Government's initiative in sending out a booklet with information about drugs is to be commended and, hopefully, this will continue to be available for a few years so that education and awareness continues to grow at all levels of Australian society.

As I conclude this chapter on silence and the world of teenagers, it is almost ANZAC day. I wish we could harness the energy our troops fought with, to keep Australia safe and free, to fight the battle to keep our teenagers safe and free from the scourge of drug abuse and severe addiction. The fight to change will need to be passionate and patriotic if we have any hope of changing the very real damage being done to teenagers, their families and our communities right around Australia. By teaching young people of today the benefits of silence and deep relaxation maybe we can help them can find their altered states of awareness in safety.

Nuts 'N' Bolts

❖ Adolescence is a very stressful time of change;

❖ We can experience transcendence in many areas of life;

❖ Transcendence is a normal drive for all of us;

❖ Allowing teenagers to experience naturally transcendent experiences may help them find such experiences without becoming addicted to alcohol and drugs;

❖ Teaching deep relaxation can give teenagers safe transcendent experiences. It can also help them manage the stress of their rapidly changing world;

❖ The rising drug and alcohol abuse in our world needs to be addressed as passionately as possible;

❖ Having loving, supportive family and friends is a key component to surviving adolescence successfully;

❖ Having quality time in nature opens adults and teenagers to transcendence.

boys *and the* magic of silence & stillness

Boys are found everywhere – on top of, underneath, inside of, climbing on, swinging from, running around or jumping to.... A boy is Truth with dirt on its face, Beauty with a cut on its finger, Wisdom with bubble gum in its hair and the Hope of the future with a frog in its pocket.

Anon
Ian Lillico: *Boys and Their Schooling (2000)*

It is a risk being born a boy. Statistics show clearly that boys, and men, are more at risk of the following:

- ❖ injury as the result of an accident;
- ❖ admission to hospital as a result of an accident;
- ❖ injury during sport;
- ❖ injury doing risky behaviours;
- ❖ failure at school;
- ❖ death or injury in motor vehicle accidents;
- ❖ offences involving criminal activity;
- ❖ imprisonment;
- ❖ being killed as a pedestrian;

- ❖ AIDS;
- ❖ death at work;
- ❖ circulatory system diseases;
- ❖ diagnosis with cancer;
- ❖ death from cancer;
- ❖ permanent disability from work;
- ❖ alcohol and drug abuse;
- ❖ suicide.

This is based on research reported in Richard Fletcher's book *An Introduction to the New Men's Health*, published by Men's Health Project, University of Newcastle (1995).

I can still remember the horror I felt as Richard Fletcher displayed graphs that showed these statistics at a 'Suicide Prevention Conference' in Sydney, in 1996. As a mother of four sons whose ages at that time ranged from seven to fifteen, I felt sick in my stomach! How was I going to keep them alive? I also knew from my counselling work that troubled boys seldom seek help, or even acknowledge they may need help.

I have always believed in the power of prayer and since that day I pray for my sons' safety and wellbeing, every single day. They need all the help they can get to survive life, first as a boy and then as a man. They are now aged from fourteen to twenty-two and three of them live together to attend university while the youngest is still at home. They are not just surviving their journeys into manhood and the world beyond, they are each conquering it. Of course, they believe this is due to their own actions, and sheer luck, whereas I believe it has more to do with my daily prayers!

Boys and Emotions

More and more, boys in our schools are becoming aggressive and violent. This is happening at younger and younger ages. The 'boys in education' expert Ian Lillico states that much of the hostility in homes and schools stems from denial of boys' feelings, and I agree with him. Many boys are also in emotionally charged situations that challenge and confuse them. Many boys are frustrated in school systems that are conditioned against boys, or that have teachers untrained adequately to meet the learning needs and styles of most boys. **Unless you can build rapport with a boy you will struggle in your ability to really connect and communicate with him**.

The whole emotional domain of feelings, theirs and others, is pretty hard for boys, and men, to understand. Irrational feelings that are hard to control cause much angst and confusion. The need for boys to mask their emotional state causes even more uncertainty and confusion.

Emotions become more confused when boys think they are their mask!!! Many boys and men bury their anger and rage over many years until this unexpressed anger turns into depression, or just bitterness, sarcasm, irritability or pettiness. Sometimes, boys 'armour' their hearts so as not to feel pain. Unfortunately they freeze out the positive feelings at the same time, which makes it difficult for them to maintain loving relationships. Adults who try to give advice to boys often unintentionally inflame emotions. If you wish to control boys' behaviours, overtly or more indirectly, then watch out! Women who question and nag their boys only add to the volatility of relationships. Boys, of course, learn to become selectively deaf very early in life and sometimes do this unconsciously; in classes they miss valuable learning opportunities.

I have noticed that the boys who cope best in school have strong auditory processing abilities, and that the reverse is also true. Auditory learners usually make up around 15% of the population. People learn in different ways. In the research by Professors Ken and Rita Dunn, from St John's University, New York, they reported the following:

❖ only a third of students remember even 75% of what they hear in a normal class period;

❖ tactile or kinesthetic learners are the main candidates for failure in traditional school classrooms;

❖ tactile-kinesthetic learners often drop out of school because they cannot focus well when forced to sit down, hour after hour;

❖ many high schools are geared to academic two-dimensional learning styles, that is: linguistic and logical. Many people involved in administration are high achievers in these two learning styles, so to them that environment works best;

❖ Most underachievers are motivated by peers to be so.

From: *The Learning Revolution,* (1997) pp349-355

Boys who are highly tactile, or kinesthetic, suffer most as teaching methods generally use auditory and visual channels of communication. This is especially true in the case of our Aboriginal children. Their culture is highly kinesthetic, using a lot of touch and movement; they are often uncomfortable with verbal communication and their auditory processing skills may be weak or undeveloped. I find them to be intuitively very strong and they know almost instantly if a new contact is comfortable with them, or is just pretending. Tactile people can be threatening for an auditory person as they will mismatch in the ways they communicate. Drawing or doodling actually helps a tactile person to stay 'on line' so that they listen better. This can be disconcerting to people who like eye contact to get feedback and validation during communication. Sensing any degree of threat in their immediate environment also stops Aboriginal children learning. I believe we would see these children have more success at school if they are taught by tactile-kinesthetic teachers, especially in the early years when the foundations of learning are built.

In my counselling experience with boys suffering despair, depression or even ideas of suicide, I find these boys often feel overwhelmed by their emotions. Emotions are unresolved, running rampant inside them. Many of these boys feel deeply flawed and a failure; they believe that those closest to them do not love them. They feel completely misunderstood.

I am often amused when parents tell me that their son has agreed to see me but says that he will say nothing. When they leave and close that door, the boy then talks non-stop. Mums and Dads are sometimes 'too close' to discuss the pain, the disappointments and the irrational fears that these boys have. It is then absolutely OK for someone else to be there to talk with them. Sometimes it may be a family member, an aunty, uncle or special grandfather. Sometimes it may be a school chaplain or a family friend who is trusted to keep confidentiality; or a sporting coach or teacher the boys believe likes them.

Just pray that there is someone who is non-judgemental, older and wiser, that they can share the confusion of their lives with; that this person will not try to take the boy's problems from them or offer unsolicited advice.

Sharing helps people understand and resolve issues that the person cannot work out by themselves. Otherwise, people can feel completely powerless to solve these perceived problems. Boys and men naturally like to be able to 'fix' things that do not work properly. I believe boys need extra reassurance that they will be able to cope, and that they will get better and better at managing the seemingly irrational emotional challenges of life. Also, we need to let them know that asking for help is a sign of strength and not a sign of weakness.

When counselling the angry and 'prone to violence' boys, I find them to have very similar issues boiling away underneath. Their mask, or defence strategy, is to wear their anger outwardly, as they feel like a volcano building up for an eruption inside them. They are seeking love, appreciation and validation even though they are being so hard to love!

Remember that testosterone levels can swing and surge from around age ten up to about twenty, sometimes with up to 800% increases. This brings a rush of energy in the body that can help the volcanos explode even more easily.

The newer therapies like Neuro Linguistic Programming, or NLP, and thought field therapies are great for boys. They can diffuse intense anger and rage without the person having to talk about it much. When I use these techniques I finish the sessions by putting the boys into a deeply relaxed state. They enjoy this because they so rarely get to that state any other time in their lives. It is a place where they can be free of talking, activity and tension.

In my experience with boys in schools and of course with my own sons, I have discovered that boys need quiet spaces to help sort out their thoughts. **I am sure that many parents and teachers overcrowd their boys with too much talk and too many questions!** It took me a while to realise that my boys settled better by playing by themselves outside, especially after a full school day. "Silence is often an excellent way of letting our sons find their own solutions rather than us imposing our own." (Ian Lillico: *Boys and Their Schooling*, 2000, p10).

How often have you sent a boy to his room, or to detention, and told him to "go and think about what you have done!" NLP suggests that this strategy may increase the likelihood of the boy repeating the experience as it is anchored in his visual memory. Giving time out to calm down and reflect is a valuable thing to do, however, the following request will bring a much more beneficial outcome: "Go and think about a different choice you could have made, that would have avoided what has happened".

Boys are not naturally as empathetic as girls. Empathy is a skill that needs to be learnt on our journey through life and creative visualization exercises can build empathy through the use of imagination.

Empathy is an extremely important emotional intelligence skill. It can help boys make better decisions when they meet personal conflict. I firmly believe boys resort to physical violence because they know no other way of 'fixing' the problem. As has already been discussed in this book, boys benefit hugely by being allowed to be boys, for as long as possible. Encouraging their imaginations to stay fresh and vivid through games and outside activities like building cubbies, making rafts and go carts, and playing test matches with the neighbourhood kids are vital to healthy releasing of excess energy; while letting them just 'do', or be. Males were created to be the hunters and defenders of their tribes, 'doing' rather than thinking about something, then analysing, comparing to others and hypothesizing. These are what come naturally to them.

Even though most boys are activity based, they still need turn off times to re-charge their batteries.

'Chilling out' in front of TV is one way that boys do this, 'tuning out' to conversation is another, or day-dreaming. Time spent alone in their bedrooms may also work. Boys often need separation time to adjust from school to being in the home environment. School and home are two different battlefields, in a sense, and the armouring needs to change. I recommend avoiding asking questions about school: did you eat your lunch? Why didn't you make your bed? And others, for at least an hour or two after school. I always tried to focus on 'watering and feeding' them as they made the school to home adjustment. I kept conversation light and funny, if possible, and I definitely became comfortable without dialogue. Even now, when the older sons come home from university in the city I give them space to read the morning paper or watch the news in peace, even though they love being home and I would prefer to be chatting, asking questions and connecting!

In the classrooms where regular relaxation and silent time occurs, the most noticeable positive benefit is the improvement in boys' behaviour and cooperation.

In classrooms, boys need more time than girls to think before answering any questions that require emotional analysis. Boys prefer quiet spaces to think, and yet they often are the ones making the noise!! Just like girls, boys learn best when they feel safe and cared for and are in environments with adults who treat them with kindness and fairness. Boys also enjoy imagination activities and respond well to the positive visions they are asked to create for themselves. These visualizations open a whole new possibility for them! I believe that boys who learn how to bring more silence and stillness into their lives manage the emotional roller coaster of adolescence better than those who have no idea about how to become quiet and still.

In an excellent study on boys in education that actually asked boys how it was for them they overwhelmingly felt girls were given a better deal in school than boys.

"In general the boys believed that girls are given more encouragement to stay at school, while many boys are actively

discouraged; told they are not clever, not well suited to work, made to feel they do not belong and that it would be in their best interests to leave."

(P7 "Perspectives from the Frontline –
What Do the Learners Say", *paper by Professor Faith Trent, Flinders University, Adelaide. 2002)*

Professor Trent also found that "the curriculum favours students who like a particular kind of work done in a particular kind of way" (p7 2002). Most boys not only found this boring, repetitive and irrelevant but also a clear sign that the curriculum was inflexible and unable to provide students with the opportunity to pursue their own learning needs and preferred learning styles. I agree wholeheartedly with this assertion and I have always found boys genuinely interested in their learning if given an opportunity. This is one of the reasons why they have responded to the use of visualization to help them improve their deep disappointment and disillusionment with schooling and learning. They also enjoy learning to think and understand how their brain really works! Glenn Capelli of The True Learning Centre in Perth Western Australia is a fantastic presenter who can teach everyone to better understand how we learn. He also uses lots of humour which is a key to reaching boys. I recommend Glen Capelli and Sean Brealey's book called **The Thinking Learning Classroom**.

The constant activity and busy-ness of boys may also lead them to create stress related illnesses in later adulthood. Heightened cortisone levels, from being in the go-go-go state, can create serious problems with anxiety and later fear based mental health problems. Constant activity can also cause sleep deprivation as winding those bodies and busy heads down for sleep is not easy. The magic of silence and stillness for boys must be taught as well as modelled because it is not a normal activity for most boys. The earlier the better!

One of the best ways to calm and quieten down boys (without words) is with gentle touch.

Back rubs, foot massages (after they have washed their feet!) will slow down these energetic souls. A friend of my youngest son stayed with us one night. He wanted a turn when I was washing and massaging feet. I gave him one of my magic foot massages and within fifteen minutes his head was back on the lounge and he was snoring! He had gone from a pretty high energy state to complete sleep in a very short period of time. When he went home and told his Mum, she too wanted to come and have a foot massage!

Please give touch a try. A hand on the shoulder. A rub of the head. A fake 'punch" on the arm. Stroking the forehead is good for calming boys if they are lying down. You obviously have to be close enough to them to do this – during their favourite TV time is often a great time. My sons enjoy a shoulder rub just anytime I happen to be standing behind them. While they are having an after school snack is often another good time to 'catch them'. The younger you start these 'rubs' the easier they accept them. Ian Lillico believes that safe touch is a critical aspect in boys' lives. Touch therapy with violent and aggressive boys is being used successfully around the world to help them relate to others better. Sometimes it speaks more loudly than words!

When boys are met with big emotional challenges, like a relationship break up, being dropped from the football team, a serious injury, death of a friend, or a car accident, know that how you support them at this time is critical. They need lots of time to work out how to deal with the problem, quite often alone, and usually somewhere safe as in their bedroom. Tell them you are there for them. However, you need guidance from them on what you can do that helps! DO NOT ASSUME ANYTHING! Offer food, endless cups of warm drinks, chocolate and make your boy's friends as welcome as possible regardless of how they look or smell. Friends are essential in their healing; do not choose to feel wounded if your son does not confide in you. Ask how you may help them.

If they are still really suffering after two weeks, without any breaks of lightness, suggest a visit to your local doctor or a counsellor. Ask them who they would prefer to see, and give them some choices. You may help by giving them the phone numbers of Youth Support, Kids Help or Samaritan Befrienders, and the phone. Maybe that is all they need! Just know that clinical depression can occur after a major upset or conflict and 'bouncing back' may need the help of someone outside of the family. If a boy has been used to using creative relaxation tapes, this is when they can work magic. Just like with Pavlov's dogs, they experience a conditioned response to the familiar tape and their minds follow the imagination on a journey away from any painful feelings. Not only that, opening to the higher self can give a different perspective and a sense of freedom from the emotional confusion and their busy inner critic. Also, they can do it alone. If they have not been sleeping properly there is a good chance they will drift off to sleep afterwards. It is like having a tonic for the soul which is on the shelf ready to use at any time.

Boys grow into men; the type of man they become is based on their experiences in childhood and in life in general. **All boys, and men, want to be loved, valued and appreciated, and they want to be in effective relationships.** Girls and women need to stop trying to change men to think like them, behave like them and be like them. If men are acting responsibly in contributing to the mortgage and helping to raise their children then allow them to escape to where they can fill their own cups with the nectar of life so that they have more to give their families. Hunting, fishing, motor bike riding trips are boy things and also men things. Let your boys and men go with love and pray silently that they come home to you safely. **Give them the spaces of quietness in the home that they yearn for** – while reading the paper, watching sport on TV or just taking a nap. Know that they are different and yet special; just like you are different and special. I firmly believe that with love, laughter, lightness and space, boys and men feel safer around girls and women. **We all win.**

Nuts 'N' Bolts

❖ It's a risk to be born a boy;

❖ Boys find it hard to understand and manage their feelings;

❖ The denial of boys' feelings can lead to aggression and violence;

❖ It is really important to build rapport with boys especially in teaching or coaching environments;

❖ Boys need quiet and space to understand and manage their feelings better;

❖ Boys need chill out time to keep up with their active lives;

❖ Being judgemental and giving unsolicited advice can increase anger and aggression in boys;

❖ Avoid asking too many questions and nagging of boys – it frustrates and angers them;

❖ Teach boys the value of quiet time and rest time when they are small;

❖ Build boys' empathy through creative visualization exercises;

❖ Safe touch is an excellent way of calming boys and of showing love without words!;

❖ Give boys and men space at home while they are doing things that they like to do alone, like reading the paper and watching sport or the news.

opening
the soul: finding
wealth *the*
within

*A soulful education embraces diverse ways to satisfy
the spiritual hunger of today's youth. When guided to find
constructive ways to express their spiritual longings, young
people can find purpose in life, do better in school, strengthen
ties to family and friends, and approach adult life
with vitality and vision.*

Rachael Kessler: *A Soul of Education*, 2000

When Aristotle and other like minded philosophers of his era began to
teach the importance of logic and rational thought, there was a huge
shift in understanding of the educated mind. From that time on, the
need to prove, beyond doubt, a fact or a concept became the norm.
Anything that could not survive such scrutiny was placed outside of
main stream philosophy and science; it was not to be taken seriously.
Only a minority of isolated scholars of wisdom stood outside this field
of thought. Even psychology, which means 'care of the soul', became
driven by a scientific mode of investigation and in time any mention of
the soul or the human spirit disappeared. Late in the twentieth century
things began to change, with the beginning of a wider acceptance

of the 'non-local' mind and unprovable phenomena; these became safe to bring out of the closet. Thanks to Abraham Maslow, Aggioloti, quantum physics and the development of new brain research, energy medicine and studies on human consciousness the world is now exposed to the broadest understanding of the human condition in recorded history. Please study the Map of the Personality in Appendix 13 to understand how the doorway to the soul – the human spirit is seated within the structure of our personality – regardless of who you are, what you believe or how you live your life. It shows that there is a layer of potential "goodness" or capacity to experience love or joy within everyone even though it may only be a tiny point of light. **Being disconnected from this layer of the personality is what I have found within every suicidal, depressed child or teenager I have seen.**

Soul in Schools

In schools, especially non-secular schools, teachers are very careful to keep all mention of soul out of classrooms. And yet, I believe every teacher knows when a soulful experience or connection has taken place. Also, teachers know when the spirit of a student has been crushed and beaten into a dark place of hopelessness and despair. Most teachers know the value of the arts, music, sports and camping in nature, for the growth and development of a whole child. In my experience in schools over a time frame of over twenty years, there has always been a search for deeper purpose and meaning within students. So, knowing that students bring their souls and human spirits to school every day should not come as a surprise. How to feed and nurture them? The challenge of education today is to change the 'spiritual darkness' of many of our young, by avoiding being too dogmatic and inflexible. **The good news is that human connectedness or building relationships with students is one of the best ways to nurture the soul of children and teenagers.**

Kessler wrote: "when schools systematically exclude heart and soul, students in growing numbers become depressed, attempt suicide, or succumb to eating disorders and substance abuse" (*A Soul of Education*, 2000). Thomas Moore in his well known book *Care of the Soul* shared a similar concern: "Fulfilling work, rewarding relationships, personal power and relief from symptoms are all gifts of the soul".

Moore also describes the symptoms of loss of soul as:

❖ emptiness;
❖ meaninglessness;
❖ vague depression;
❖ disillusionment about marriage, family and relationship and life in general;
❖ a loss of values;
❖ yearning for personal fulfilment;
❖ a hunger for spirituality.

In my work with children, sometimes as young as five, and especially with teenagers, disillusionment and despair with their lives and our world are epidemic. These young people have many of the symptoms described in *Care of the Soul*. To me, this is a message that whatever we have been doing until now must be improved upon. Parents and teachers need to learn ways that nurture the hearts and souls of our children and teenagers. We also need to be mindful that we do not 'throw the baby out with the bath water' as there are some things that we do now that are beneficial and helpful. Bringing the magic of silence and stillness into our young people's lives is a key way of allowing them to reconnect to their souls and spirits.

Rachael Kessler explores seven gateways to the soul for students in schools. I believe an understanding of these gateways can help every parent and teacher better understand how to nurture, encourage and inspire healthy growth, of spirit and soul. These gateways are outlined in the following pages, but I encourage you strongly to read Kessler's book as she explores each of the gateways in depth, anecdotal evidence and insight.

The Yearning for Deep Connection

How Can a Person be Lonely
How can a person be lonely
When surrounded by friends?
How can a person be lonely
When taking and making calls?
How can a girl be lonely
When their parents are near?
I am lonely.
I am alone.
Because no-one sees my thoughts
No-one understands them

I am lonely
I am alone
I am dead.

Melanie Pan MacMillan, Sydney, 1992, p302.

This poem by Melanie Woss is believed to have been written on the night she committed suicide.

The first gateway of a yearning for deep connection should come as no surprise; it is a key component of any resiliency program. When we talk of deep connection we need to be mindful that it comes in many ways. Kessler explores the following forms of deep connection.

❖ Deep connection to self
❖ Deep connection to another
❖ Deep connection to community
❖ Deep connection to lineage
❖ Deep connection to Nature
❖ Deep Connection to a Higher Power

As adults, we can help our young people build different levels of connectedness. We can do this without touching on the one that is less appropriate in our non-secular schools, the deep connection to a Higher Power. I cannot see why any parent or education department representative could have any objection to the first five levels of deep connection. A healthy connection in any one of these is important and will build a strong sense of connectedness, a key element in the development of a healthy soul.

Larry Dossey in his book *Healing Words* (1994) explored the concepts of love, empathy and connectedness: "Empathy, compassion and love seem to form a literal bond – between living things" (p111). This bond occurs even with spatial separation. One fascinating story involved a dog called Bobbie who was relocating from Ohio to Oregon with her family. On the way the dog was lost and the family had to continue on to its new location. Almost three months later, Bobbie appeared on the doorstep of the family's new home. The scientists studying the case believed that the deep emotional connection between the dog and its family was sensed on a non-local mind level and enabled the dog to follow that sensory trail until it found its family. The dog's path was later tracked and found to be almost a straight line!

Let us never underestimate the human yearning to feel loved and connected. It does not have to be by family and it does not have to be in human form. It just has to exist in a very positive way so that the psyche senses it. People of all ages can then feel they belong on our earth and that people care about them. By addressing this gateway alone, we may be able to reduce youth depression, suicide and substance abuse. Thankfully all resiliency studies recognise the need for connectedness as a key protective factor that helps keep our kids and adults alive.

The Longing for Silence and Solitude

Soul cannot thrive in a fast paced world because being affected, taking things in and chewing on them, requires time.

Thomas Moore: *Care of the Soul*, 1994, p286.

This is the second gateway that Kessler describes. The longing for time spent in silence and solitude is unrecognised by many in the Western world. Yet the positive impact that 'the magic of silence' has on countless children and teenagers validates the longing for silence and solitude. Stressful lives are often devoid of this. The whole focus of this book is on the value of silence for the healthy nurturing of soul and human spirit. On the way, it promotes better learning and mastery of life.

Ian Gawler in his book *Meditation Pure and Simple* (1996) wrote: "The real secret to all this is that this balance is found in a state of inner silence – simple silence. By restoring our natural state of balance there is a flow on effect. Soon we experience physical balance and good health, emotional balance and poise, mental clarity and confidence, and spiritual harmony".

Both Moore and Gawler have discovered the enormous benefits of silence and stillness, from quite different searches. Thomas Moore began his search deep within the Catholic Church, through years of study of theology, philosophy, mythology and psychology. Ian Gawler began as a veterinary surgeon. He developed bone cancer which led him to discover the power of self healing through meditation and an awareness of the principles of personal healing and wellbeing on a holistic level.

In my work with teenagers, I encourage them to create their own sacred place, somewhere that has significance to them. If they belong to a church they may choose to use their church, or the gardens of the church. If they have no recognised faith, I encourage them to remember a place in their childhood where they felt safe and protected and then to recreate a similar place. Sometimes boys enjoy being up a tree. Sometimes their place will be a beach or in a quiet place in amongst nature, a bit of bush or some trees. For country kids or teenagers it may be a place on their family farm. This becomes a place they can go to in solitude and have time out from the world. Over time, the place brings more and more comfort and peace. It is where they can then go to clear their heads, work through an issue or just calm down.

A chosen sacred place works best if it has somewhere to sit and a familiar view. I am fascinated how many kids and teenagers have such a place, and yet they forget to go there when they are troubled. In time, this becomes a place that brings forth answers to deep questions, to the point that the answers are anticipated. The familiarity brings immediate comfort. Being in nature in stillness is healthy for the body and the mind. If you don't have a place like this, find one soon!

> *"The most beautiful thing we can experience is the mysterious. Recognition of the mystery of the universe is the source of all true science. He to whom emotions are a stranger, who can no longer pause to wonder and stand rapt in awe is as good as dead; his eyes are closed."*

> Albert Einstein
> from p162 *Infinite Mind* by Valerie Hunt

The final key point to remember with the gateway of silence and solitude is that silence and stillness can be the doorway that allows connection to the other gateways. It is, therefore, important in the healthy integration of a whole child.

The Search for Meaning and Purpose

> *Encoded in our genetic material, just as surely as the colour of our eyes or hair, is a call to greatness, an impulse to experience that part of us which lifts us above the mundane and touches upon the divine.*

> Andrew Auw: *The Gift of Wounding*

Being in a state where you feel like there is no purpose or meaning in life can be a frightening place. Humans have a deep drive within to be of value, worthy to self and others. So often people, of all ages, struggle with how they perceive their purpose for being on this planet. Children question these issues of meaning and purpose much earlier than in my generation, or in preceding generations.

How can adults answer these questions while they are still searching for their own answers? For as many years as I can remember I have lived by the belief that everyone has something to offer the world, that is unique and like no other. This something has the potential to make the world a better place. Somewhere, we hold the seeds to gifts and potentials that can grow into being this positive gift to the world. As the carers and guardians of our children we have a responsibility to help them find their gifts too. I feet it is responsible to sow this seed of hope and possibility into young children because without it they may struggle with the search for meaning for the rest of their lives. Focusing on making small changes to make the world better seems like a sensible thing to do, rather that allow kids to compare themselves to famous athletes, sports stars or world leaders. To be a participant in life is a key part of the message, while knowing how deep and irrational many children's fear of failure is in their minds. Being thoughtful or considerate of others makes the world a better place. Writing music, performing, being a part of a school play, acting as a mentor for a younger student can also make the world a better place.

When I first read work on multiple intelligences I realised that what I was reading could help us as parents and educators to help children find what gifts they have hiding inside them. Kids who have high levels of logical-mathematical and visual special intelligences have much better aptitude in further education in the areas of maths, science, accountancy, economics, architecture and building than someone with high levels of linguistic and musical intelligence. We find, early in primary school, that some of these gaps, or advantages depending on how you view them, become obvious. We need to reaffirm to children that they can find competency in life – the search is the interesting part, especially if school has been boring or possibly too challenging.

The kids with a high level of tactile or bodily-kinesthetic intelligence need to follow school pathways that allow them to do things and be practical. It is interesting to note that despite the wonderful discoveries of brain research and preferred learning styles, the pinnacle of education, our universities, still use lengthy lectures as a key component in further education. When lectures are delivered by strongly linguistic-logical-mathematical teachers with sometimes a strong foreign accent, it must challenge many students to learn, or to 'stay on line'. Let's hope we soon see changes that recognise the new information and understandings – especially in teacher training institutions!

We are all 'wired' to search for meaning in all facets of life. The children of today are questioning and searching for meaning, and how they can contribute to the world, as a big part of their search or quest. When we feel we have contributed in some way then we can genuinely feel our own self value and worth; our self esteem is lifted and we have a sense of being a meaningful part of our world. From my work in a local prison I know that unless we can build a sense of a potential to make the world better in some way into the psyche of offenders, then their chances of re-offending will always be high. Without sowing the seeds the crop cannot grow and the harvest will never happen.

The Hunger for Joy and Delight

What's the hardest thing about skydiving? The ground.
Why do tigers eat raw meat? Because they can't cook.
Why do birds fly south in winter? Because it's too far to walk.

This is not just a hunger that we are observing in our homes and schools, it borders on starvation! Joy and delight are food for the soul and yet there are many people who have never experienced it. So incredibly sad!

The key moments I recall when I shared joy and delight with students were after moments of challenge. One was on the school canoe trip when we almost lost two boat crews out to the ocean, due to an unexpected storm. The students setting up camp in trying conditions worked hard to create an environment that felt safe. There was no division between students and teachers. After many hours of concern and worry, out of the darkness appeared the missing students, with two very exhausted staff. What followed was such an amazing, spontaneous celebration that it caught many of us by surprise. Life was so exquisite and valuable! This experience was bonding, so powerfully unfolding, that we all hugged and danced like young children at a Christmas party when Santa arrived. The joy flowed into a feeling of deep connection and that evening when we tried to sleep in wet sleeping bags we slept close with arms around each other. As I write I still feel the emotion within me of that special evening.

As a culture, Australians are depreciatory in their ability to celebrate!

Maybe it's the English 'stiff upper lip' that is still present in many of our genes! We tend to hold back on spontaneous joy as though it is something we need to contain. Our children are also conditioned at an early age to 'settle down' when they are too excited; yet they are in the throes of joy or delight! I know that without the laughter and lightness in my home, shared with my boys and their many friends, we would all have experienced more pain and challenges as we journeyed through childhood and the teenage years. Experiences of deep connection can bring forth joy. Music, singing, dancing, awesome moments in nature can result in joy. The simple experiences of being remembered, acknowledged, validated or thanked all bring forth a bubbling of joy within us, even if we are alone.

At the National Speakers' Conference in Sydney, in March 2003, I was able to experience joy and delight after participating in a drumming session, shared with over one hundred and fifty fellow participants. We were led by two drummers on stage – called Motivational Non-Speakers – and it was quite amazing how they were able to lead totally novice drummers, each with our own drum, to a state of unity and sheer delight – WITHOUT A WORD BEING SPOKEN! Rachael Kessler explains that "a wild inventiveness that stirs souls can release a current of joy" (*The Soul of Education*, 2000, p86).

Another source of spontaneous joy is the deep connection to some of Mother Nature's wonders. The star filled night when seen a long way from city lights can be breath taking. Amazing dawns and sunsets can have the same effect. I was surprised when I was visiting the Grand Canyon in 1998 that at sunset, all the people gathered became silent and reverent as the sun sunk towards the horizon. It was a moment of awe that touched those present and made us silent – even young children. It was so amazing that my sister and I decided to get up early next morning and watch the sun rise over the canyon. This was worth it, even though it meant we had to get out of bed at 4.10am to be there in time!

My sons are very used to being drawn outside when there is a stunning full moon, interesting cloud formations, or cloud bursts as the sun's rays shine through the clouds; I call them God clouds! And while my boys think their mother is 'missing a few kangaroos in the back paddock', I know they have enjoyed some of the moments too; sometimes, they get me to 'come and watch' too. I have seen the brilliant sparkle in their eyes when they return from a surfing trip to say that they were joined in the surf by a school of dolphins, or that they saw a whale close by – sheer joy and delight that is provided free of charge by Mother Earth.

The old Lakota was wise. He knew that Man's heart away from nature becomes hard; he knew that lack of respect for growing, living things soon led to lack of respect for humans too.

Lakota Chief Luther Standing Bear

The Power of Laughter

I am a firm advocate for bringing more laughter and lightness into classrooms and homes. Laughter has some wonderful instantaneous benefits:

* transformation of emotional states;
* creating endorphins of well being;
* enabling of key coping skill, especially for boys;
* providing an anti-bullying strategy;
* encouraging lightening up for the 'all too' serious;
* bonding when shared in groups;
* building inclusivity and connectedness;
* releasing tension and stress;
* as a key element in effective communication, especially in close relationships;
* anti-violence – a powerful antidote.

If there is laughter in your home or classroom, then you are building heart connections that fill the emotional cups of the young people present. There are a few teachers at our local government high school who use laughter in their classrooms and I know that without them my boys would not have been able to be as successful in high school as they were. Without that lightness and bonanza of non-academic pursuits they would have pulled out of the academic streams. They probably would have struggled more to find fulfilment and an authentic life direction.

The Creative Drive

About School
He always wanted to say things. But no one understood.
He always wanted to explain things. But no one cared.
So he drew.
Sometimes he would just draw and it wasn't anything.
He wanted to carve it in stone or write it in the sky.
He would lie out on the grass and look up in the sky
and it would be only him and the sky and things that needed saying.
And it was after that he drew the picture. It was a beautiful picture
He kept it under the pillow and would let no one see it.
And he would look at it every night and think about it, and when
it was dark, and his eyes were closed, he could still see it.
And it was all of him, and he loved it.
When he started school he brought it with him. Not to show anyone,
but just to have it with him like a friend.
It was funny about school.
He sat in a square, brown desk like all the other square, brown desks
and he thought it should be red.
And his room was a square, brown room. Like all the other rooms.
And it was tight and close. And stiff.
He hated to hold the pencil and the chalk, with his arm stiff
and his feet flat on the floor, stiff, with the teacher watching, watching
And then he had to write numbers. And they weren't anything.
They were worse than the letters that could be something if you
put them together.
And the numbers were tight and square and he hated the whole
thing.
The teacher came and spoke to him. She told him to wear a tie
like all the other boys.
He said he didn't like them and she said it didn't matter.
After that they drew. And he drew all yellow and it was the
way he felt about morning. And it was beautiful.
The teacher came and smiled at him "What's this?" she said
"Why don't you draw something like Ken's drawing,
Isn't that beautiful?"
It was all questions.
After that his mother bought him a tie and he always drew
airplanes and rocket ships like everyone else.
And he threw the old picture away.

*And when he lay out alone looking at the sky, it was big and blue
and all of everything, but he wasn't anymore.*
*He was square inside and brown, and his hands were stiff, and
he was like everyone else.*
*And the thing inside him that needed saying didn't need saying
anymore.*
It had stopped pushing. It was crushed. Stiff. Like everything else.

Source Unknown

This poem was handed to a grade 12 English teacher in Regina, Saskatchewan. Although it is not known if the student actually wrote it himself, it is known that he committed suicide two weeks later. It resonates with every high school student I have ever read it to, as it touches something deep inside them. The image of the young boy drawing 'like everyone else' is something I have witnessed with my English classes when doing creative writing. By high school, students have worked out how to 'play it safe' and to stay within the 'norm', to curb their natural creativity and originality. It took me the better part of a year to get students to let themselves run free in creative writing, to write with passion and authentic expression. I still have the end products in a box where I keep special things.

Importance of Non-Academic Activities

Training in art therapy has made me familiar with the information and insights that can be gained from using the arts to express our inner worlds. A simple example of an insight took place in a preschool one of my sons attended. As I came to collect my son one afternoon, I noticed a painting on the wall of a little girl with blonde hair who was covered in red spots. The teacher said it was really interesting as the little girl painted that on the Friday and on Sunday she broke out in chicken pox!

In my work with children I use drawings to externalise emotional problems, so that the children can then 'throw them away'. I use some colours to represent negative feeling states that children want to release. The use of symbolism and colour makes it easier for children to share their inner pain as they do not have the emotional maturity required to describe their feelings. They often call feelings "yukky" – and that can be 'yukky – sad' or 'yukky –angry'; the colours they use to draw the yukky feeling tell me which it is.

I am a firm believer in art for the art's sake. By this I mean allowing children to draw, paint, create music or make their own plays or dances with free expression. They seldom are allowed free expression without adult limitations. This is such wonderful food for the soul.

My youngest is currently fourteen. In his first week of school this year, he rushed home with sparkling eyes (which usually have something to do with being surfing). He was so excited about a craft class he was taking. Joy of creating in a class with a safe and non-intrusive teacher has lasted for two terms! I was so thrilled to see his sheer enjoyment and to know it was happening in year 9 – a year commonly known as the nightmare year for boys!

Creativity has the power to feed the heart and soul of our kids, teenagers and adults. The art of creating is also benefited by silence and solo time. Preparing the mind by using creative visualization is demonstrated by many primary and secondary teachers to be helpful. It helps calm and settle the brain in an optimal state for being creative.

Just imagining being creative can bring "juice" into the heart and soul – actually doing it is even better as we have something to show for it.

The Urge for Transcendence

As I have already covered 'Transcendence and Adolescence' in a previous chapter, I would like to affirm the value of mini transcendent experiences for children. Children who become immersed in non-structured play and in imaginary games enjoy a sense of freedom from the ordinary. The same freedom can be experienced in short visualizations that use the imagination.

There is no place in our schools for use of any relaxation activity that has any hypnotic, mystical or deeply religious intention. The exercises that are appropriate are simple diversions from the busy world we live in. They open to an imagined world full of calmness and perceived freedom from threat. Exercises that open students to a more positive vision of themselves and their school achievements are also appropriate and safe. Beyond that, we are venturing into unchartered waters that may create conflicts on philosophical and educational levels in our schools.

The Need for Initiation

The final gateway that Rachael Kessler explored in her book *The Soul of Education* is that of the need for initiation, or a 'rite of passage'. Simply put, this means the need for acknowledgement and recognition of the major life changes that children go through on their journey from babyhood to adulthood.

David Oldfield, an American specialist of adolescent rites of passage and the importance of ceremony, wrote the following in the Sydney Morning Herald, in April 2003: *"Trying to warn adolescents off rash or suicidal behaviour doesn't work. Adolescence has always been a time for risk-taking and more traditional societies were wiser than ours in that they created fitting tests and challenges for teenagers to face, and turned these into rites of passage."*

Bill Kerewsky, editor of TEAM, an early adolescent magazine in the United States, puts it: *"We are the only civilization in history to have created a whole category of people (adolescents) for whom we have no real use. In times not long gone fourteen year olds helped on the farm. Now however we have protected them out of jobs and relegated young adolescents to the roles of pizza consumer and video tape junkie."*

As a civil celebrant I am very aware of the power of ceremony in anchoring or opening us to major life changes. However, I know the difficulty that faces us, as educators and aware parents, of convincing our teenagers of the benefits of implementing 'rites of passage'. These can improve the physical, emotional and mental well being of emerging young adults, called adolescents. Joseph Campbell's metaphor of the 'hero's journey' is one that many teenagers are able to grasp. This is an excellent starting place for the teaching of the importance of the need for initiation.

Most of us live according to a significant life metaphor and it is a key focus in NLP when helping an individual understand why they are living a limited life.

Another excellent example of a metaphor that may help teenagers is Bryce Courtenay's poem from his small book *Recipe for Dreaming*:

Dare Your Genius to Walk the Wildest Unknown Way

Go where you've never been before. Dream up a destination, a path to follow, a wildest unknown way, over rocks and scrag, across high hills where the winds bite cold with malice, through deep mysterious valleys where the wild things roar

and echo and rumble and stamp and hiss great clouds of steam from
their terrible huffing ways.
Dream the impossible dream and start walking towards it .
On the way you will be beaten up, chewed, spat out, mauled, ripped apart, given up for lost.
Quite soon you'll learn what it feels like to be beaten up, chewed, spat out, mauled, ripped apart and given up for lost. This is called experience and it's very, very valuable in life, because what you mostly learn from is that you were more afraid of what might happen than what did happen. Most successful outcomes are achieved by calling a series of conventional bluffs.
One bright sunny morning you'll discover that the wild and the unknown way you once took is carpeted with moss and strewn with tiny flowers. It has become a familiar path, a well trodden direction which has put you miles ahead of anyone else and much, much closer to achieving your once impossible dream.

Bryce Courtenay *Recipe for Dreaming*

This chapter was always going to be risky. Nothing alienates people faster than divisions of belief, especially of a spiritual or religious nature. However, we all know when we have fed our soul or have had an experience that has touched something very deep within us.

I was blessed to have a wonderful Dad who taught me that he never found God within a church and yet he knew there was something much more powerful than he that defied description. Rather than try to define the 'IT', he simply shared those moments with me. These were moments like seeing the first born lamb in June, the first turning of the plough to show the chocolate rich earth in autumn, the stillness of the frosty morning before the sun peeped over the hills, the first breaking rains after a long hot summer, and the quiet gratitude for the blessings of a family gathered to share a celebration at Christmas. I was blessed to have been guided by one so wise.

Silence and stillness has the potential to open one to the mysterious, to the immeasurable and to the unknown. The alienated teenager who finds the world a spiritual void with an absence of meaning and purpose is a person at risk. If I have one main desire from writing this book is that at least one young person may choose life over the choice of creating their own death. They may give it just one more go to find a sense of value – to experience the joy of feeling connected and loved. They may take a position of power and ask someone for help in their dark night of the soul experience. I pray that in some quiet magic moment some light may flow into their being giving them hope. It happened to me all those years ago when I tried to take my life. No-one came when I called – just a gentle ray of sunshine through a window and I then saw everything a little different.

Nuts 'N' Bolts

❖ Nurturing our kids hearts and souls as well as their minds and their bodies is educating the whole child;

❖ There are seven gateways to the soul of education:
   1. The Yearning for Deep Connection
   2. The Longing for Silence and Solitude
   3. The Search for Meaning and Purpose
   4. The Hunger for Joy and Delight
   5. The Creative Drive
   6. The Urge for Transcendence
   7. The Need for Initiation

❖ Spirituality rather than religion is what the young are questioning;

❖ Alienation and disconnection can be overcome with education for the whole child;

❖ Silence and stillness is often a doorway to the other gateways to the soul of education.

getting started for parents: creating the magic of silence in your home

The best place to get started is straight after conception! The research done by Masaru Emoto in his book "Messages from Water" on the molecular structure of water shows that sound and thought forms can alter the molecular structure of water. The changes can be positive or negative as showed clearly in the amazing photographs in his book. These amazing photographs can also be seen on the web at "www.wellnessgoods.com/messages.asp". As the human body is made up of around 70% water then the impact of toxic thoughts and sounds on the forming baby can be devastating. So soothing sounds and music are very beneficial for unborn babies.

When I have been working with children and teenagers who are struggling with low self worth and self esteem, there is a core negative belief that supports their low sense of personal value that seems to influence other negative self beliefs.

Using techniques from kinesiology it is possible to find that this core belief was formed while still inside their mother's uterus. A very common core wound is one based on being unwanted and sometimes women find themselves to be unexpectedly pregnant and this negative thought form can be absorbed into baby's perception and maybe mistakenly sensed by the baby as being about them personally.

This belief then becomes part of the unconscious belief system of the child, and so that unconsciously he or she will filter their life experiences through this core belief. It is extremely hard to feel love and acceptance of oneself authentically while believing that you were unwanted. To ensure that a child feels valued and wanted from as early as possible it can be helpful during pregnancy for the baby to hear both parents offering love and positive messages of welcome. Also beautiful music and plenty of nature sounds helps to create positive molecular structures for the new baby.

Peaceful silence is also really beneficial for babies and young children even though they can sleep through noise in family environments. Yelling and screaming at young children causes tension in their nervous systems and makes them fearful and nervous even if they do not show overt signs of any problems. The real problems appear later when they are frightened of making mistakes or become driven to being perfect especially at school. Taking risks is very much a part of healthy education and many children with learning problems also have core beliefs that do not support them being capable at school.

Tips to Build Comfort for Children With The Magic of Silence and Stillness

Most of these are covered in the main body of the book. However I am aware some very busy parents may just turn directly to this section.
1. Be comfortable with quietness yourself and model it.
2. Use quiet tonality when speaking or making requests of children.
3. Use soothing music in the home.
4. Spend time in quietness like taking a nap together.
5. Use massage and safe touch to calm hyper active little ones from birth
6. Connect children to nature. Make sure children become mindful of:
   - ❖ sunrises and sunsets;
   - ❖ first rains of winter;
   - ❖ first leaves falling in autumn;
   - ❖ full moons;
   - ❖ rainbows;
   - ❖ power of the wind;
   - ❖ cloud and star watching;
   - ❖ warmth of gentle sunshine;
   - ❖ fun of paddles and water falls;
   - ❖ beauty of seeds and flowers;
   - ❖ trees in their shapes and sizes.
7. Turn the TV off more often. Limit its use.

8. Limit time on the computer as it heightens the brain's energetic state.
9. Take walks and swims often – it settles spikey energetic fields.
10. Create family quiet times. Meals with no TV. Eat outside often.
11. Encourage reading for pleasure.
12. Read to hyper active children to calm them.
13 Try aromatherapy using oil burners. Check you are using calming essences like sandal wood, lavender or a mixture specially made for calming.
14. Clearing the aura or ruffling. This above the body method works really well for ADHD kids before you try them with creative visualizations.
15. Stroking gently the forehead, the back or the feet. N.B. Diffuse position.
16. Bush flower essences or Bach Flower Remedies for calming. See information about Bush flower essences in Appendix 12.
17. Sensory Activities like play dough, clay modelling or building with sand. Finger painting, painting back fence with coloured water, blowing bubbles outside.
18. Try to use humour to diffuse energy. Do the unexpected!!!
19. Milo Time!!! Maybe it is an illusion however making a warm cup of milo for both of you can soothe frazzled nerves!!!
20. Encouraging time out in their own room, bed or beanbag… not as punishment!!!
21. Use imaginary stories like Maureen Garth's "Starbright" or "Moonbeam."
22. Use creative visualization tapes or nature music in their own rooms especially as they prepare for sleep. Repetition helps build pathways for calmness in the mind. Also positive messages can be set in the unconscious mind.
23. Hug and reassure often. Practise more kindness and compassion.

Special Tip for Teenagers

Remember that they are at a crossroad in their life between childhood and adulthood. All of the tips for children are worth a go as the child part of them is still strong no matter how tall or big they are. Just buy them a tape or CD and say that it helps with sleeping. Many teenagers are seriously sleep deprived.

Encouraging them to join a yoga class or tai chi or a class that teaches breathing is helpful. You,of course will have to pay and take them!!!! The benefits will be worth it. Please do not nag or try to manipulate them.

Mean Mums

We had the meanest mother in the whole world!

While other kids ate candy for breakfast, we had to have cereal, eggs, and toast. When others had a Pepsi and a Twinkie for lunch, we had to eat sandwiches. And you can guess our mother fixed us a dinner that was different from what other kids had, too.

Mother insisted on knowing where we were at all times. You'd think we were convicts in a prison. She had to know who our friends were, and what we were doing with them. She insisted that if we said we would be gone for an hour, we would be gone for an hour or less.

We were ashamed to admit it, but she had the nerve to break the Child Labor Laws by making us work. We had to wash the dishes, make the beds, learn to cook, vacuum the floor, do laundry, and all sorts of cruel jobs. I think she would lie awake at night thinking of more things for us to do.

She always insisted on us telling the truth the whole truth, and nothing but the truth. By the time we were teenagers, she could read our minds.

Then, life was really tough! Mother wouldn't let our friends just honk the horn when they drove up. They had to come up to the door so she could meet them.

While everyone else could date when they were 12 or 13, we had to wait until we were 16.

Because of our mother we missed out on lots of things other kids experienced. None of us have ever been caught shoplifting, vandalizing other's property, or ever arrested for any crime. It was all her fault.

Now that we have left home, we are all God-fearing, educated, honest adults. We are doing our best to be mean parents just like Mum was. I think that's what's wrong with the world today. It just doesn't have enough mean mums anymore.

Unknown Author

getting started for teachers: creating the magic of silence & stillness in the classroom

"What if...

...we created a safe and caring environment in our school?

...everyone respected individual differences and the diversity of our cultures?

...our teachers designed learning experiences to reach students who learn in different ways?

...students became responsible for themselves and each other?

...we knew how to educate all of our students for success in the 21st century?

... our families became more actively involved in the education of their children?

...we could awaken a love of learning in everyone?"

P15 *Tribes* By Jeanne Gibbs

Teaching children the benefits of the magic of silence and stillness will help all of us involved in the schooling of our children achieve the vision as painted by Jeanne Gibbs.

There are many things that teachers are already doing in our classrooms that improve the emotional well being of children. The summary can be found in Appendix 5. One activity that I believe that can be used more for students of all ages is the use of story telling.

There are many books that have stories that contain "teachable moments" for children and teenagers. I thoroughly recommend the Chicken Soup for the Soul series written by Jack Canfield and Mark Victor Hansen. These books accompanied me to many relief classes and students often wanted to hear the same story over and over again!

Another excellent one especially for teenagers is "Taste Berries for Teens". This is written by one of the subscribers of Chicken Soup and is published by the same company. It covers topics that all teenagers can relate to and it has stories written by teenagers. Teenagers hate being lectured to by adults and story telling provided it is based on real stories, and real events and people is an excellent way of sowing seeds of possibilities and choices for them if they ever find themselves in a similar situation.

To really know the benefits of deep relaxation if you are unsure buy yourself a CD which has a guided visualization on it and do it between five and ten times in a two week time frame. It doesn't have to be mine! I recommend the 15 minute guided visualizations as they are the ones you will use most in class due to time restrictions.

Experience it yourself and then you can convince your students.

The many teachers who have brought relaxation into their classrooms have given me feedback on how much more they are enjoying their teaching. Students respond to the calmer rooms and often work harder so that they can be rewarded with a visualization! It is wonderful to see the high numbers of pre-school teachers coming to the Magic of Silence trainings and seminars. If children are introduced to quietness and calmness early in their life, it will make it so much easier for the teachers that follow. The overwhelming feedback from teachers is that classroom behaviour changes and conflict is reduced. This can happen with just two fifteen minute quiet sessions a week using the creative visualizations on A Little Time Out CD.

So how do you introduce the Magic of Silence and Stillness into your Classroom?

Before you begin to bring this magic into your classroom please ask yourself :

- ❖ **What is my main intention in doing this?**
- ❖ **List three benefits that I believe can be achieved by bringing the practice of more silence and stillness into my classroom.**

❖ **What is most important to the majority of your parent body?**
1. happy kids
2. improved school achievement
3. less conflict at school
4. improved self esteem for students
5. more resiliency skills for later life
6. better thinking skills

Rank these and then work out how the magic of silence will address the key issues of concern. Then create a parent meeting followed by a letter of explanation on the new strategies you would be implementing so that interested parents may follow the new direction at home. Also follow appropriate school administration communication channels.

What parent does not want the above listed benefits for their child?

There are five key areas that cover the cognitive and emotional benefits of the Magic of Silence and Stillness. There is a Diagram of these benefits in Appendix 13 for ease of photocopying.

Benefits of Magic of Silence and Stillness

1. Imagine Time
This concept is based on the brain based research that has determined that the brain learns best in a state of "relaxed alertness." The imagination can be a powerful tool when preparing for creative activity including creative problem solving. It can imagine that it is already being very imaginative and not only will the child's physiology change to a positive state their unconscious mind will follow the directions given in the visualization or quiet preparation time. Both prepare the child to become more creative and original.

The short visualizations I have created on the Little Time Out CD were created for this reason. They are simple, set in nature and allow a calming of the mind before the learning experience starts. Beach Bliss, Moonlight Magic and Flight Fantasy are the titles.

2. Calm Time
This is when the class synergy or group energy is scattered maybe following lunch, or following an emotionally unsettling experience like a world crisis, a local unexpected death or maybe a school fight that involved many students.

This can be as simple as lights dimmed (or coloured lava lamp on) with quiet music playing and silence. Students come in and rest, read, or lie down and listen to a 10 minute visualization. It helps if they have their own pillow and can lie on the floor. Then do some deep breathing to bring them back into full awareness and some stretching and grounding activity is also important to bring the brain on line for whatever class activity you have planned.

This can also include **Pause Time** – reflection time after a lesson, a day or even at the end of term.

> *"You may use this time to clear your mind or to notice what you are feeling or thinking right now, or to digest what has happened in your last class. You may use this time to reflect, to pray, to remember something or to set a goal for tomorrow or you may just rest."*

Reflection is an opportunity for reviewing one's learning, emotional state or creating a new possible vision for the future. In silence we can reflect without interruption. Please consider the following quote from Dr John Edward's key note address at The Excellence in Teaching Conference at Burswood, Perth WA in January 2002.

The title of his address was "The Things We Steal from Children."

> *"If I speak of individuals but present learning as if they are all the same.*
> *If I am never seen to reflect and reflection time is never provided.*
> *If we never develop a vocabulary to speak about our thinking.*
> *If I signify that there are always right and wrong answers.*
> *If I never openly respect their thoughts.*
> *If I never let them persevere with the difficult and complex.*
> *If there is no time to explore.*
> **How will they get to know themselves as a thinker?"**

> *(Part of a poem co-written by Dr John Edwards,*
> *Professor of Education, University of Queensland,*
> *with his wife Sandy Russell. 1996)*

3. Focus Time

This can also be called think time as it involves preparing students for focused thinking and or concentration for new learning. This is when we remind students that brains need to "switched on" – use "Hook ups" to settle quickly, then maybe use brain buttons, and other brain gym activities.

Then command all magic brains to be fully alert and in high energetic state. This will direct unconscious minds in your classroom to be ready even if students do not follow on a conscious level.

This can also include "**Wait Time**" – to avoid stress and to allow students time to formulate a response to a question give students this time. For deeper answers try think-pair-share, or think-write –share. Recall questions need less "wait time" because students either know it or they don't. Remember boys need more time with emotionally based questions.

" *We are preparing our bodies and our brains to be in a place of relaxed alertness for our next activity so that we are able to positively concentrate and focus on the task at hand. You can put your worries in a worry basket so they do not distract your magical brain during this time.*"

4. Rest Time

Rest Time can be seen to be that valuable time when we honour the brain's need to downshift or download – take time to sort and store. Or maybe we can honour times when students are genuinely tired.

Nap Time – sometimes especially towards the end of term students are simply tired and a quiet time usually in the afternoon can be greatly appreciated.

Or maybe the class has worked really hard and diligently and they deserve a reward – this can be it! Cheaper than chocolate!

"*This opportunity is for a ten minute nap because at this time of the term many of us are feeling a little tired. Simply follow your deep breathing and then take time out from the world. You may sleep, rest or simply lie still and listen to the music or just daydream.*"

5. Dream Time

This aspect of quietness and silence is about expanding the imagination. Lord David Putman believes we have become children's dream stealers. (Centre of Excellence Conference Perth at the Burswood,2002) I agree with him wholeheartedly. This is a time to expand the imagination. It expands the mind and can create positive visions for the future not just for individuals – also for our world. How can we create a peaceful world without first visioning it?

We all must have unrealised dreams hidden inside us that will help us propel ourselves forward in life. This is not about goal setting. This is about imagination and possibilities!

Follow on activities after relaxation and quietness can include:

Journal Time – a quiet time to ponder on the following questions before journal writing is important. The shy students often do not want to share thoughts and feelings out loud and the journal gives them a chance to do this.

> *What did I do well today?*
> *Is there anything I wish I had done differently?*
> *What was hard to think or talk about today?*
> *Was this topic a good one for me?*
> *What challenged me today?*

Drawing Time – A visual diary can be as important as a journal. It is simply for drawing in or doing cut outs from magazines or somewhere to put photographs.

Emotional Cleansing

On a transpersonal level emotions can be symbolically represented by colours and with intention and breathing emotional energy or tension in the nervous system can be released quite gently.

Red – *anger, frustration, resentment*
Orange – *emotional hurt*
Brown – *disappointment or feeling let down*
Grey – *sadness or grief*
Black – *fear*

Use outward breaths to let go of these colours and breathe in a colour that represents calmness or happiness and feeling loved. These are the colours that children have taught me most commonly represent these feelings. With younger children they can choose a colour that represents feeling "yukky."

How to Introduce Relaxation in the Classroom

My first suggestion is to ask students who enjoys being shouted at or having loud voices around them? Then explain the reason why a silent sound signal will be of benefit to the class. Demonstrate the raised hand method. When students see you raise your hand they raise theirs and close their mouth at the same time until everyone notices the hands and becomes quiet. Give them an opportunity to make other suggestions on a silent sound signal. I had one group design a red flag!!!!!

My second suggestion is that you must have convincing reasons why silence and stillness is important. Read my list of concerns regarding young people and children from my introduction and that you wish to create a safer classroom that improves learning and general wellbeing. Ask them the same questions I gave for parents

1. **Begin with the rationale for its use**
    a) The brain is amazing and loves quietness
    b) Develops both sides of the brain
    c) By using both sides of the brain the brain becomes more effective and learning improves
    d) Visualization can improve creativity, increase athletic ability, improve memory and accelerate learning
    e) Improves thinking and problem solving
    f) Gives the brain "down-shift" time
    g) Improves classroom environment and inclusion of students
    h) Helps positive self esteem and self worth
    i) Builds connectedness and resilience
    j) Creates safer friendlier classrooms.
    k) Happy kids learn better

2. **Give the guidelines that apply during quiet time:**
    ❖ Put a Do Not Disturb Sign on the door – kids can make it!
    ❖ Dim the lights – do not totally darken the room
    ❖ Choose one of three positions if doing imagination techniques
      1) Lying down
      2) Taxi Driver Position
      3) Head on Folded Arms
    ❖ Students must keep eyes closed
    ❖ No talking and no touching or disturbing others
    ❖ It's OK to fall asleep but not to snore. (Snoring student will have a gentle hand placed around their lower leg to bring them out of deep sleep.)
    ❖ It's OK to go on your own imaginary journey
    ❖ Raise your hand silently if you need assistance
    ❖ Create "detour fantasy" just in case
    ❖ Create a totally tactile, fun detour fantasy like falling into a vat of warm chocolate or diving into huge tub of warm custard. This is just in case a unpleasant image appears like nanna's funeral. I have never had a student

who needed assistance and sometimes I use their detour
fantasy as a calming two minute diversion from noisy
room!!!!

❖ Do not compare, judge or analyse others. Very rarely do
students share their visualizations as they are very vivid
and normal class activity happens soon after

❖ If there is an interruption treat it like a TV commercial

❖ Allow others to "come back" without interruption – some
take longer than others

❖ Always be confidential about other's experiences
NB: Avoid doing relaxations before a break or
immediately after a meal. After lunch at school seems to
be OK

❖ **Begin with simple breathing techniques and teaching
grounding**

Simple Relaxation

1) Breathe in for a count of 1 and out for a count of 2, then go up by
doubling until you are breathing in to a count of 6 and out to a
count of 12. Then go back down until the 1/2 count.

2) Begin with three big deep breaths and then tense the muscles in
your legs for a count of five then relax. Then tense the muscles in
arms the same as your legs, then relax. Then your neck muscles
and finally your face muscles, then relax.

3) Try to sit quietly for two minutes…you may have your eyes open
or closed. Have your desk clear before you begin. Try silently
repeating "I am resting", or "I am calm".

4) Breathe out tiredness and breathe in energy. Breathe out worries
and breathe in peace. Breathe out tension and breathe in
calmness.

5) As you breathe in deeply focus on the air coming into your nostrils
…and NOTHING else. It takes practise however relaxation can be
this simple.

6) The Star Prelude from Maureen Garth's books is probably the
best way to introduce a guided imagination exercise for young
children. As people have difficulty with the guardian angel idea it
is still effective to do use the prelude until the Guardian Angel is
introduced. If that bothers you or your parents create an imaginary
creature who protects you and keeps you safe.

Also the worry tree tends to work better as a worry basket because the sticking into the tree bothers some kids.

7)   When children 'come back', ensure you get them to stretch and breathe to bring their full awareness back. As you bring them back, remind them that they are special, unique, loveable and capable, and that they are on our earth to make it a better place in some way.

Precautions When Using the Guided Relaxation

❖   We all have hidden feelings and regrets. Sometimes when we become still these can surface spontaneously. This can sometimes happen to students. Reassurance is often all that is needed. If a student seems concerned refer to school psychologist. Remember do not be frightened of emotions – let them pass through. Encourage students to breathe out any sadness or anger and then breathe in their positive colour if anything unpleasant should come up.

❖   Avoid bringing your own personal beliefs or spiritual truths into this practice. If you are teaching in a religious school be mindful of using appropriate words and images that meet your faith's beliefs. This is simply a matter of semantics.

❖   If students feel they have seen or spoken to a deceased relative during a guided relaxation reaffirm how amazing the imagination can be. We know that real or imagined images appear real to the brain so this is actually quite appropriate.

❖   If you are stressed and tense this will come through to the students. Use someone else's tape or CD so you can benefit too.

❖   " We risk the half-hearted teacher who tries to implement cutting-edge strategies in a mechanical way that breeds even more cynicism and alienation in our young." Rachael Kessler. That is why I am giving the background and depth that exists behind the magic of silence and stillness.

❖   Prepare parents by explaining the benefits you are seeking – do not do it without them being aware as it may create scepticism and doubt.

❖   Some students may still need to be withdrawn if parents are not comfortable with their children participating.

❖   Be clear about **your intention** for bringing relaxation into your classroom and you will feel more at ease with what and how you are doing it. Remember the KISS principle!

❖ Do not express negativity about children going to sleep....some children are very sleep deprived.

❖ Build the sense of safety and security in your class before you attempt the longer guided relaxations.

❖ Remind students of the importance of feeling unique and worthwhile while they are relaxed. It takes at least 8 positive praises to undo each negative one a child receives.

❖ Hyperactive students will find it quite difficult – please persevere. Try some of the techniques from the Calming Children chapter. Keep them close to you. Maybe keep your hand gently on their forehead. These are the children who benefit the most from the magic.

Go a Little Further

When your mind says *"I can't"* but your heart says *"yes, you can"*…
Go a little further…

When your mind says *"I have done all I can for these kids"*
But your heart says *"tomorrow is a new day"*
Go a little further…

When your mind says *"There are too many kids who really don't care"*
Find a few each day who do care and…
Go a Little Further…

When your mind says *"I just don't have the support I need,"*
But your heart is still full of determination,
Go A little Further…

When you wonder why you are here, remember…
that one student whose eyes sparkled when he finally figured IT out…
or that one student whose smile told you that you touched her life…
or that one student who never cared, but one day cared a little bit…
Go a Little Further…

For when we reach out a little more, we hold onto a possibility…
For when we try one more time to connect, we create a possibility…
For when we go a little further…
We find the power within us to handle all we need to handle…

We live in a world of have to's, should do's and ought to's
and sometimes we lose our focus, sometimes we become discouraged,
we wonder, can we ever make a difference?
we wonder, does it really matter? AND
we wonder, can we really help our students find their real potential?

Alone, we can only do so much, together… imagine the possibilities…
for if each one of us plants the seeds of success,
the seeds of hope and the seeds of kindness
in the hearts and souls of children everywhere

Then maybe without even knowing it
we may create a beautiful garden of possibilities
With flowers of all kinds in
a wonderful rich tapestry of colour and texture.

Teresa Huggins & Maggie Dent "Esteem Plus" 2000

Epilogue

Our world continues to be a place of conflict and uncertainty. It will continue to be so while we seek out the differences between people, cultures and countries. There is no one right way of living or being. Maybe if we searched for the sameness within others there would be more harmony.

There is a Buddhist saying that goes like this:

> "When there is peace in the heart, there will be peace in the home, there will be peace in the country and there will be peace in the world."

I believe that with more stillness, silence and sometimes solitude our world would be a better place. Children and teenagers from England, to Canada, to New Zealand and America are struggling to come to terms with this world of immediacy that we now live in. I know our children benefit from slowing things down a little, becoming quieter and calmer and I hope and pray that as a result of this book, more quietness will find its way into the lives of at least one child or teenager somewhere in our world. Homes and schools can be safer, calmer and better places to spend the precious moments of our lives and the lives of our children.

Everyone yearns for relationships that care and nurture them, for safe environments that allow for authentic growth and cooperation and for a way to make a positive mark on this world. Everyone yearns for real connectedness with themselves, others and our world. With knowledge on how to care for hearts and souls, as well as minds and bodies within our homes and schools we may turn around the social crisis facing children and teenagers in our developed nations. There is a potential within every child ever born and we need to keep searching for better and more effective ways of ensuring that this potential is realised – no matter what!

Maggie Dent
August 2003.

Appendix

1. Accelerated Learning Technique for Struggling Readers – Dr Gerald Jampolsky

2. Accepting Myself – Maggie Dent

3. The Perfect Student Fantasy by Dr Beverly Gaylean

4. Our Magic Brain – Maggie Dent

5. Activities that Encourage Emotional Intelligence

6. Seven Gateways to the Soul of Education by Rachael Kessler

7. Creating the Vision for Safe Caring Classrooms

8. Resiliency and Mental Health – Attributes for Well Being

9. Creative Visualization and Jack Canfield

10. Brain Gym Relaxer

11. Summary of Benefits of Magic of Silence and Stillness

12. Bush Flower Essences That Help Calm Children

13. Map of Personality

14. Bubble Summary

Appendix 1

Dr Gerald Jampolsky, Director of the Centre for Attitudinal Healing in the US created the following guided visualization for remedial readers at the elementary level.

Accelerated Learning Technique

Let your body find a comfortable position lying down or sitting up. Take three long slow deep breaths and let yourself become more relaxed with each breath.

There is no-where to go and nothing to do except become more and more relaxed with each breath that you take... Let yourself open and close your eyes until you become more comfortable with having them closed... notice that with each breath you become more... and... more relaxed.

Now imagine you are getting into a lift in a tall building. As you look above the door you can see the number 1 is lit up. After the door closes and the lift begins to ascend one floor at a time. You can see the numbers above the door changing from 1 to 2 to 3 and so on... You can feel yourself becoming more relaxed as the elevator goes higher and higher... more and more relaxed as each floor goes by... until you are finally at the tenth floor.

Now imagine that you could reach up to the top of your head and find a zip than runs from the front of your head to the back of your head. Go ahead and unzip the zip and gently remove your brain and place it on the ground in front of you. Now imagine that you have a hose in your hand and begin to wash your brain with the hose... get rid of all the dirt and grime in your brain... wash out all the painful memories of having difficulty with your reading... wash out all the old ideas in your brain that interfere with your reading... wash out all the phrases and ideas like "I can't... ", "It's too hard... ", "I'll never be able to do it... ", "I'll try... If only... But... ". These words and phrases only create negative pictures in your mind that will make the past repeat itself... As you wash your brain you are replacing these words with "I can... Reading is simple and fun... I like to read... Every day I get better and better at reading... "

You are washing away your negative belief system about your ability to read.

You are replacing it with a new one that will help you to read easily and quickly. You will be surprised and delighted to see how easily you can read now that you have washed away these old ideas from your brain… you will be pleased with yourself and feel proud…

Now very gently reach down and pick up your clean brain. Notice how white and clean it is now. All the negative thoughts and memories have been washed away. Now very gently put your brain back in your head and zip the zip back up… well done…

Now imagine that you are sitting at your desk at school… think of your most favourite subject in the whole wide world, the thing you most like and are most interested in… Now imagine you are writing a small book about this subject… think of all the things that you would write in such a book… realise how easy it would be for you to write the book… you know all the words and you know how to spell the words easily. You are really enjoying writing the book… it is fun and exciting…

Now imagine reading the book you have just written. You can read all the words easily because they are all the words which you have written earlier.

Imagine that you are reading the book aloud so that you can hear each word… listen to how your voice sounds… you are able to read each word fluently and easily… See yourself flipping the page over as you go on to the next page. Notice how the pages feel in your hand… They are smooth and crisp. Notice how the cover feels. It is stiffer than the pages. You are feeling positive and really confident as you read because you know that you can recognise, pronounce and understand all of the words without any problem… you can feel a big smile come on to your face as you continue to read easily…

Now imagine that you are sitting in front of a giant TV screen. On the screen you can see yourself reading a book… you can see yourself reading this book with pleasure and ease because there is a big smile on your face… You are reading successfully, fluently and without effort. All of the words come very easily to you. Just watch and listen as you see and hear yourself reading easily

… Now imagine that there is is a door right in the middle of your giant TV screen and you can open the door and walk right into the program of you reading… you then step into the image of yourself reading and climb into that body and become that person… you are now the person who is reading easily… you are the clever person who can read well, without effort, and you feel really good and you have an even bigger smile on your face…

Now take this picture of yourself and put it into your blood cells… then see these magical bloods cells taking that positive picture of you reading really easily and well to your organs and to the tissues of your body... your brain, your muscles, your bones and your skin... You have now become one with the picture of yourself reading...

Now return to the lift and see yourself descending in the lift to the bottom floor.

When you reach there the lift will open and you will return to the lobby... you will see yourself step out... becoming aware of your body again... take a few deep breaths and when you are ready you may stretch and open your eyes.

Appendix 2

Accepting Myself

Age: 12-17 years old   **Time: 5-10 minutes**

Close your eyes and focus on your breath. Take three long slow deep breaths inward through your nostrils and outward through your mouth allowing your body to gradually relax and release tension from the body. Then as you breathe in… and out… allow your feet to become relaxed… and then your legs become relaxed… then your back… then your shoulders then finally your arms and shoulders.

As you continue to breathe in and out gently and quietly allow your head to become quieter and more relaxed… allow your mind to run free… allow thoughts to come in and simply flow through and away.

Pretend that you yourself are floating away from this room for a short time… to a place where you will feel really safe and comfortable. This place may be a place in nature, or maybe a place you have visited on holiday… any place where you can feel really good about yourself…

When you get there enjoy the warmth of the sunshine and breathe that warmth into your body… allow that warmth to feel like a loving feeling and allow the whole body to feel that way.

Now allow yourself to see yourself as perfect exactly as you are… then see yourself as a great and loyal friend… Now see yourself as a caring and loving member of your family… and as a positive participant in your school environment… Most importantly see yourself as being really happy with who you are… See yourself at ease doing well with your school studies, with any sport you play,… any other passion you have like dancing, skating, playing music… especially see yourself happy with your own company… let that feel really good… Really let your body experience the unique joy of being you… because there is only ever going to be one of you… you are unique and valuable and here to make a positive difference to our world. You are one of a kind… how special is that?

Continue to experience the warmth of the sun and breathe in the peace and well being of being you… Pause… 1-2 minutes

I am now going to call you back into this place in this time. I want you to bring back with you the feeling of happiness and well being with being you… and I want you to keep it with you all day… and I want you to especially take it home at the end of the day to your home and family…

I will count to three and at 3 you will open your eyes , stretch and slowly come back into this present awareness.

Maggie Dent 2000

Appendix 3

The following guided imagery(slightly adapted) was used by **Dr Beverly Gaylean** (Director of the Confluent Language Teaching Project in the Los Angeles City Schools) to help students in an inner city high school Spanish class reduce negative behaviour (lateness, disruption, put downs etc.) and increase positive behaviour (improving communication with other students, oral and written participation in learning activities etc.)

The results of the intervention (daily use during the first 5-7 minutes of class for a period of 3 months) showed highly positive results. Students exhibited increased attentiveness, increased involvement with the lessons being taught, an increase in the number of supportive interactions among the students themselves and an increase in supportive responses to the teacher.

The Perfect Student Fantasy

"Close your eyes for a few minutes and relax. Let yourself take a deep breath. As you breathe in, imagine yourself taking in all the most beautiful, wholesome, helpful good energy around you... As you breathe out see yourself breathing forth any tension, worry, doubt or negativity you might be feeling... Do this again... slowly breathe in... and take all the good that is around you... As you breathe out rid yourself of any doubt, or negativity that you might be feeling... Take another deep breath, once again breathing in the good around you. This time as you breathe out feel yourself floating away... floating gently from the room... Float away now to a place where you would really like to be. This is a favourite place where you feel really good and safe... go there now... float gently to this place... When you get there just enjoy being there... While in this beautiful place imagine looking at the sky and see the sun and feel the warmth... the glow... ask the sun to descend nearer to you making you feel warm and very comfortable... very safe and secure... Notice how the sun warms you but doesn't burn you... The sun feels very friendly today... now call the sun to enter your body through the top of your head. See how it lightens you.makes you feel weightless. Gradually it descends through your head... releasing all the tension in your eyes... jaws... neck... shoulders... arms... hands... chest... stomach... thighs... legs... and all the way down to your feet. Now notice how light you feel... experience your own warmth and brilliance... experience the good that is you... Now see yourself as absolutely perfect... capable of achieving anything you want. You have the ability to succeed. You can see yourself as perfectly capable exactly as you are. What do you look like as perfectly capable? How are you behaving? How do others think of you?... see yourself as perfectly capable... now see yourself as perfect in this class. You have all the knowledge... all the ability to be a perfectly capable student. It's up to you. What do you look like as a perfectly capable student in the class? What are you doing in the class?

Silently and inwardly to yourself tell yourself. "I am perfectly capable... I am perfectly capable... Others in my class are here to help me be perfectly capable... I am here to help myself become perfectly capable..." Say this to yourself three more times silently...

Now that the sun has descended through you, you can now begin to draw it back up through your body from your feet up... slowly bring the sun up your legs and up through the trunk of your body until the neck and upwards through to the top of your body. As the sun leaves your body through the top of your head you will feel really light and bright... kind of glowing all over. Enjoy this feel of being totally connected to yourself... Take a deep slow breath... hold it for a few moments and then slowly let it out and feel yourself gradually floating back into the room. Gently bring your self fully back into this room while still feeling really light and positive... when you are ready open your eyes and enjoy being you in a room full of other perfectly capable positive students...

Then stretch and finish with a smile...

N.B. You can modify this visualization to suit your needs. Maybe a little shorter for younger children. The key positive beliefs to reinforce are:

- ❖ I am lovable and capable
- ❖ I enjoy my schoolwork... my reading... my maths...
- ❖ I am a special person no matter what other people say or do to me
- ❖ I am clever in my own way
- ❖ I am important and valuable to myself and others
- ❖ I love and appreciate myself exactly as I am
- ❖ I find learning fun
- ❖ I am happy to be me
- ❖ Even if I sometimes make mistakes I am still lovable and capable
- ❖ I am on this earth for a very important reason
- ❖ I have gifts and talents and I really like who I am
- ❖ My world is safe

Appendix 4

Our Magic Brain

Age: 10 – adult **Time: 5-8 minutes**

Students can use this exercise when preparing or studying for a test or assessment task. It is helpful to prepare the brain for memory recall and problem solving.

Close your eyes and take three long slow deep breaths and relax the physical body. Then silently tell the body to relax more and more with each outward breath.

Bring your attention to your head and then inside your head to your brain. This amazing part of the human body is quite complex and yet totally magical. From this centre all stimuli and information that all of your senses are constantly collecting, are directed. This magical brain holds vast stores of information and knowledge. It actually pulses with this information.

Pause for a moment and think back through your life to moments when you have learned something or maybe mastered a physical activity that previously you could not do... Can you remember making sense of letters and pictures and learning to read?... Maybe you can remember understanding how to do division in Maths... or maybe learning how to write freehand in such a way that people could actually read it? In your brain is stored everything that you have heard, read, studied, seen, done, touched or smelled!

Silently and inwardly I want you to feel very proud of your magic brain. Thank your brain for being so brilliant and helpful... and I want you to feel very clever that you have such a magical brain inside your head!...

Now I want you to silently tell your brain that you wish to recall any information needed to do really well on this assessment task... Imagine that your brain is feeling relaxed and alert... ready to look into the file where you have stored all the information you have stored for this test or task... Finally tell your brain that you totally trust it to perform well for you...

Choose a colour that represents feeling positive and happy... imagine that you can take three big breaths of that positive colour and breathe it into your brain turning it from white to your favourite colour... Now your brain is switched on and ready to help you complete the learning task in front of you.

I will slowly count to three and at 3 you will open your eyes feeling relaxed, alert and very ready to start your learning task...

Maggie Dent 2002

Appendix 5

Activities that Encourage Emotional Intelligence

❖ Paired sharing

❖ Role play and drama

❖ Reflection time

❖ Time for lightness and laughter

❖ Journal and Poetry Writing

❖ Drawing and Creative Arts

❖ Circle Talks

❖ Creative Imagery

❖ Dancing and Singing

❖ Feedback Times

❖ Story Telling

❖ Play

❖ Creative problem solving

❖ Regular quiet, solo time

❖ Safe, nurturing touch

Maggie Dent 1999

Appendix 6

Seven Gateways to the Soul of Education

By Rachel Kessler Soul of Education

1   The Yearning for Deep Connection

2   The Longing for Silence and Solitude

3   The Search for Meaning and Purpose

4   The Hunger for Joy and Delight

5   The Creative Drive

6   The Urge for Transcendence

7   The Need for Initiation

Appendix 7

Creating the Vision for Safe Caring Classrooms and Homes

Key Possibilities are :
- ❖ A sense of belonging
- ❖ A sense of being cared for
- ❖ A place of safety
- ❖ A place where respect is encouraged and modelled
- ❖ A place that is positive and encouraging
- ❖ A place where everyone is committed to cooperation and collaboration
- ❖ A place where diversity is appreciated
- ❖ A place where a love of learning is nurtured
- ❖ A place where everyone is heard and understood
- ❖ A place where people are responsible for themselves
- ❖ A place where choices are made as a result of effective communication
- ❖ A place that encourages the growth of potential in each student
- ❖ A place that encourages and accepts personal excellence
- ❖ A pleasing environment with a receptivity to learning
- ❖ "Smiling faces" and optimistic individuals
- ❖ Care and consideration as intended outcomes
- ❖ Acceptance of diversity
- ❖ A place people look forward to coming to
- ❖ Shared decision making
- ❖ Understanding of life enhancing communication
- ❖ Clear direction, goal setting and sense of purpose and relevance
- ❖ A commitment to the pursuit of excellence
- ❖ A place where praise and encouragement is shared and valued
- ❖ An environment where there is a positive thought field present
- ❖ A place where kindness and compassion have replaced criticism and punitive punishment.

Maggie Dent Albany 2001

Appendix 8

Resilience and Mental Health

Factors identified by **Mind Matters** that build resilience and mental health and wellbeing for children and adolescents.

1. Connectedness

2. Relationship with caring adult

3. Support, belonging, role models

4. Self Esteem

5. Belief in own ability to cope

6. Handling the demands of school

7. Sense of Control

From *Mind Matters a Mental Health Promotion Resource for Secondary Schools.* www.curriculum.edu.au/mindmatters

Creative Visualization

The human psyche needs times of quiet for the development of a positive inner world, for time to reflect on current reality, and for the nurturing of a healthy emotional intelligence.

Creative visualization is important in the development of the imagination, giving the brain time to rest and renew and it is also helpful when settling group energy. In the long term the use of creative visualization will help in managing stress, building self esteem and self worth, building positive self images and the creation of safer, more caring environments especially in our homes, schools and institutions.

Jack Canfield of Self Esteem Seminars

CV can achieve a wide variety of objectives:

- ❖ Enhancing self esteem
- ❖ Expanding awareness
- ❖ Facilitating psychological growth and integration
- ❖ Evoking inner wisdom
- ❖ Increasing empathy
- ❖ Increasing memory
- ❖ Building imagination
- ❖ Facilitating optimal performance
- ❖ Evoking a more positive attitude
- ❖ Accelerating the learning of subject matter
- ❖ Stimulating whole brain integration

With regular use 2-3 times a week research has clearly shown that students exhibit:

- ❖ increased attentiveness
- ❖ increased involvement with the lessons being taught
- ❖ increase in positive social interactions among students
- ❖ increase in supportive responses to teacher
- ❖ increase in reading skill (with Accelerated Learning CV.)
- ❖ increase in self esteem
- ❖ increase in emotional breaks in behaviour
- ❖ parents noticed improved behaviour, less tension

From Facilitator's Skills Seminar
1998 Santa Barbara, Cal, USA.

Appendix 10

Brain Gym Relaxer Hook Ups

Hook ups are done by
1. First crossing one ankle over the other, whichever feels most comfortable.
2. The hands are crossed, clasped and then inverted. In a balanced way this activates the sensory and motor cortices of each hemisphere in the brain.
3. While in this position rest your tongue on the roof of your mouth, behind the teeth ie. The hard palette. This action brings to mind the mid brain which lies right behind the hard palette.
4. Breathe a few deep breaths.
5. This configuration connects emotions in the limbic system with reason in the frontal lobes, thus giving an integrative perspective from which to learn and respond effectively.

Hannaford 1995 Dennison 1994

This is great before a test or assessment or activity that causes you to feel anxious.
- Like a difficult phone call.
- Like needing to make a complaint about something.
- The calmer you are the better chance you have of getting a favourable outcome.

Appendix 11

Summary of Benefits of Magic of Silence and Stillness

❖ Creates optimal conditions for learning

❖ Opens mind to creativity and better problem solving

❖ Builds emotional intelligence and competency

❖ Improves energetic fields both – individually and group

❖ Nurtures the inner world and the human spirit

❖ Builds resiliency skills for life

❖ Improves ability and capacity to think

❖ Lessens fear – imagined or real

❖ Creates opportunity to "be" rather than "do"

© Maggie Dent 2003

Appendix 12

Bush Flower Essences

Ian White, a naturopath with a Science degree, a Diploma of Naturopathy and Diploma of Biological Medicine and a fifth generation Australian herbalist, has created a range of herbal remedies that are completely natural. These remedies are being used by doctors, pharmacists, veterinarians, naturopaths and therapists to assist people in healing emotional domain of the physical body.

Discover the power of the Australian Bush....

What are Flower Essences?
Flower Essences are not therapeutic drugs – but work on the mind, body and spirit and are obtained by extracting the healing vibrational quality from the most evolved part of the plant – the flowers. They work on an emotional level, harmonising negative feelings and belief patterns, held in the subconscious mind.

How long have flower Essences been used?
For thousands of years Australian Aboriginals have used flowers to heal emotional imbalances and physical injuries. Flower Essences were also used in Ancient Egypt, as well as Asia, Europe and South America.

This system of healing was rediscovered and popularised sixty years ago by Dr. Edward Bach with his use of English flowering plants. Naturopath Ian White has further developed this method using plants from all over Australia. Ian grew up in the bush and was taught from an early age the power of Australian plants. He has spent many years travelling Australia researching and developing a range of 65 specific Essences.

There are specific essences that help with calming of overcoming aggression and anger. Some of these are listed below.

Black Eyed Susan – helps with irritability, intense impatient behaviour

Flannel Flower – to encourage gentleness of touch, expression of feelings

Jacaranda – poor concentration skills, scattered

Kangaroo Paw – poor social skills, aggressive behaviour towards others

Dagger Hakea – anger, resentment, bitterness to those close
Mountain Devil – anger, jealousy and hatred generally
Rough Bluebell – deliberately hurting or manipulating others
Illawarra Flame Tree – for rejection – real or imagined
Red Helmet Orchid – deepens relationship with father, helps in
    dealing with authority figures
Slender Rice Flower – prejudice towards others after bad
    experiences with one or many of another race, culture or
    religion
Hibbertia – rigid, inflexible attitudes
Southern Cross – blaming others, victim mentality
Five Corners – because of low self esteem they can be very
    needy and act or behave to get attention even if it's negative,
    builds self esteem, self love and acceptance
Bush Fuchsia – coordination, brain balance, speech and reading
Green Spider Orchid – for nightmares or "night terrors"
Grey Spider Orchid – for extreme fear and terrors, particularly
    irrational
Crowea – brings balance on all levels

There are combination essences that are used to improve focus and concentration, to help with adolescent issues, improving confidence and also a wonderful emergency essence that can be administered every 10 minutes until a person feels better.

Calm – Focus Combination or Calm – Emotional Balance Combination

    From Bush Flower Healing by Ian White
    For availability check out web site : www.esteemplus.com
    Or the Ian White Web site www.ausflowers.com.au

Map of the Personality

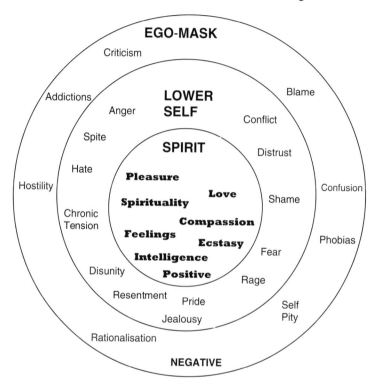

This symbolic map of the personality is adapted from John C. Pierrakos. Sometimes when we communicate we think we are being honest, when in reality we are speaking from our mask. We have to acknowledge that we have all levels of our personality and that sometimes we can feel disconnected from our spirit.
The voice of your spirit is much quieter than the voice of your ego.
Sometimes, your spirit will try to communicate to you silently through your senses or your feelings.
ALWAYS listen to your senses and your gut feelings...Check experiences and choices with your spirit. IT KNOWS YOU BEST.
Trust yourself

Appendix 14

Magic of Silence and Stillness

IMAGINE TIME

Prepare for creative exercise
Problem solving
Group work

CALM TIME

Settling energy fields
Breathing
After lunch

FOCUS TIME

Concentration training
Energise brain buttons
Encourage brain to be present and alert for new learning

REST TIME

Following busy activities
Near end of term
Brain reward time for effort

DREAM TIME

Creative positive visions for future for self, class or world.
Vision with emotion.

© Maggie Dent 2003

References and Bibliography

Andreas, S. & Faulkner C., (1996) **"NLP: The New Technology of Achievement"** London, Nicholas Brealey Publishing.

Arrien, A. (1993) **"The Four Fold Way – Walking the Way of the Warrior, Teacher, Healer and Visionary."** San Francisco: Harper SanFrancisco

Bennett, Barrie., et al (1991), **"Cooperative Learning"** Canada. Educational Connections,

Bernard,B. (1991) **"Fostering Resiliency in Kids: Protective Factors in the Family, School and Community."** Portland, OR. Northwest Regional Education Library.

Biddulph, Steve., (1994) **"Manhood"** Lane Cove, NSW., Finch Publishing .

Biddulph, Steve., (1997) **"Raising Boys"** Sydney. NSW. Finch Publishing.

Boyd, Julie., (2000). **"Active Learning and Cooperation"** (1998)**"Creating Resilient Youth"** www.workingfutures.com.au

Brendtro,L., Brokenleg, M & Van Bockern,S. (1990) **"Reclaiming Youth at Risk: Our Hope for the Future."**Bloomington, IN: National Education Service.

Burns, E Timothy., (1991)**"Our Children Our Future"**, USA Marco Polo Group

Caine, RN and G., (1997) **"Education on the Edge of Possibility."** USA, Association for Supervision and Curriculum Development.

Canfield, J., & Wells, H.C., **"101 Ways to Enhance Self Concept in the Classroom."

Canfield, J., & Siccone, F., (1995**) "101 Ways to Develop Self - Esteem And Responsibility."** Simon and Schuster, Mass. USA.

Canfield, Jack & Hansen Mark Victor,(1995) "**A 2ⁿᵈ Helping of Chicken Soup for the Soul"**, USA, Health Communications Inc.

De Bono, E., (1999) **"New Thinking for The New Millenium."** Penguin, London.

Biddulph, Steve., (1994) **"Manhood"** Lane Cove, NSW., Finch Publishing .

Biddulph, Steve., (1997) **"Raising Boys"** Sydney. NSW. Finch Publishing.

Buzan, Tony (2001) **"Use Your Head"** Great Britain, BBc World Wide Ltd

Dossey, Larry MD.,(1993) **"Healing Words: The Power of Prayer and the Practice of Medicine."** San Francisco, Harper San Francisco.

Dossey, L., (1989) **"Recovering The Soul"**, USA., Bantam.

Dryden,G and Vos J, (1997) **"The Learning Revolution"**, The Learning Web, New Zealand.

Elias, Maurice .J., Tobias, Steven. E., & Friedlander, Brian. S.,(1999) **"Emotionally Intelligent PARENTING"**, USA, Doubleday.

Garth, Maureen,(1996) **"The Power of the Inner Self: A Book of Healing"** Australia, Harper Collins Publishers.

Garth , Maureen, **"Starbright" " Moonbeam" & "Earth Light" Meditations for Children.** Australia. Harper Collins Publishers.

Garth, Muareen, **"Inner Garden", "Inner Space",** Harper Collins Publishers

Gawain, Shakti (1978) **"Creative Visualization"** San Raphael, Cal, USA. Whatever Pub.

Gawler,Dr Ian., (1996) **"Meditation Pure and Simple",** Melbourne, Aust, Hill of Content Publishing Co.

Goleman, D., (1995) "**Emotional Intelligence."** New York. Bantam.

Goleman, D., (1998) **"Working with Emotional Intelligence."** London, UK, Bloomsbury.

Goleman, D., Boyatzis,R & McKee, A. **"The New Leaders."** London, UK, Little, Brown.

Greer, A., (1990) "**Meditation Workbook."** Brunswick, Victoria. David Lovell Publishing.

Grose, M., (2003) **"Why First Borns Rule the World, And Last Borns Want to Change it."** Sydney. Random House.

Hunt, Valerie. V., (1996) **"Infinite Mind: Science of the Human Vibrations of Consciousness",** California, USA, Malibu Publishing Company.

Kline, Nancy (1999) "Time to Think: Listening to Ignite the Human Mind." UK, Ward Lock Book.

Lillico, Ian. (2000) **Boys and Their Schooling**

Lillico, Ian (2002) **What Makes Boys Act Like Boys**

Mind Matters 2000 **"A Mental Health Promotion Resource for Secondary Schools".** Commonwealth of Aust. http://www.curriculum.edu.au/mindmatters

Moore, T., (1992) "**Care of the Soul; A guide for creating depth and sacredness in Everyday life.**" New York, Harper Collins.

O'Donohue John, (1997) **"Anam Cara: Spiritual Wisdom from the Celtic World"** London, Bantam Press

Parry, T., & Gregory,G.,(1998) **"Designing Brain Compatible Learning"** Australia, Hawker Brownlow Education.

Pearsall, Paul Dr.,(1998) **"The Heart's Code: Tapping the Wisdom and Power or our Heart Energy"** New York, Broadway Books.

Pelzer, D (2000) **"Help Yourself: Celebrating the Rewards of Resilience and Gratitude. "** USA, Penguin.

Pinker, Steven (1997) **"How the Mind Works"** London, Penguin Press.

Rosenburg, Marshall .B., Ph.D (2000) **"Nonviolent Communication"** USA, Puddle Dancer Press.

Rozman, Deborah (1975) **"Meditating with Children : The Art of Concentrating And Centering."** USA, University of the Trees Press.

Shadel, Doug& Thatcher, Bill (1997) **"The Power of Acceptance"** USA , Newcastle Publishing.

Shone, Ronald, (1984) **"Creative Visualization: How to Use Imagery and Imagination For Self-Improvement"**, London, Aquarian Press.

Wilson, Paul (1995) **"Instant Calm"** Australia, Penguin Books.

Woss, Melanie., (1992) **"Melanie"** Sydney, NSW, Pan MacMillan Publishing.

By Maggie Dent

A Little Time Out

This CD has three short visualizations for individuals and groups – excellent for beginners and classrooms. The guided visualizations are Beach Bliss, Moonlight Magic and Flight Fantasy. These are also great for very busy people who only have time for 10 minutes of relaxation!

Beautiful music by Robert J. Boyd.

Rainbow Balance

This CD includes a guided visualization and calming music composed and performed by Will Upson. This visualization uses the colours of the rainbow to calm and relax the body and the mind and is used by people all over Australia enhancing sleep and reducing pain and worry.

My Safe Place

This CD is a great for creating a familiar place in the imagination where you can take time out from the world, to rest, reflect and renew oneself. This has been used successfully with ADHD and individuals suffering from anxiety disorders.

Music by Will Upson.

Secret Mountain

This guided relaxation will not only help you to relax deeply – it will also help you connect to your heart. The walk up a mountain is an important metaphor that symbolises the conquesting of life challenges and the search for the highest and best within us. This visualization also reconnects you to Mother Earth. Just as She can be a powerful source of comfort and wisdom, you too will feel comforted.

The music that accompanies Secret Mountain has been inspired by Ki Energy Grand Master, Tae Yun Kim, a sacred piece of music. Gently and quietly, come and visit The Secret Mountain.

Music by Paul Gilman (USA).

School Mastery 1

This CD contains three visualizations for students aged 7 to 17 to improve school achievement by changing attitudes and internal representations of potential. The three are Accepting Myself, My Best Report Ever and I Can Read Easily. This CD is helping students achieve better results and create more enjoyment for learning – especially good for low achievers.
Music by Robert J. Boyd.

School Mastery 2

This CD is for students in the last years of school or those doing tertiary studies. This is often a time of increased stress, major decision making, and life changes The three are Accepting Myself, Chilling Out and Life Mastery. The Chilling Out visualization is a serious stress busting one especially for around exams or moments of challenge. The Life Mastery has been created to help teenagers and young adults make positive and optimistic life choices and possibilities in their life.
Music by Robert J. Boyd.

The Endless Journey: A Message for Every Child Ever Born.

This inspirational message has been created to give children and young adults a simple explanation of life and our purpose here. It is only a 10 minute message that is accompanied by another beautiful piece of Robert J. Boyd's music.

Musical Notes

Will Upson: Will was a former big band man who moved to the country in the 1990's. He is a brilliant composer who has written unique books to support the musical education of students. He created Stress Free Music and composed special music for Rainbow Balance while playing golf! He is widely respected and admired in Western Australia. Will's music is also an important half of My Safe Place. A very special gentle man.

Robert J. Boyd: Robert is a very gifted composer, musician and physician who learnt early in life that different emotions could be created in people through different sounds and styles of music. His music has been very much a part of my therapy work for the last few years as it has a healing potential of its own. Robert has been very generous with sharing his gifts with me in the creation of my Little Time Out CD as well as my School Mastery CDs. Robert's many CDs are listed on his web site. www.robertboydmusic.com

Paul Gilman: Paul is a musician, composer, performer and a pioneer in electronic music who has been creating simply divine music for many years. We met at Jack Canfield's FS Seminar in Santa Barbara in 1998. His passion for the merging of sounds to create harmonious states is unique and very special. Paul has risen to new heights by composing sound tracks for movies and his unbelievable compositions with nature, especially our beloved whales and dolphins. Paul has given me permission to use a very special kind of music on the Secret Mountain. Paul's other CD's are listed on his web site. www.paulgilman.com

TIME OUT SERIES	12+
Rainbow Balance Meditation	CD
My Safe Place	CD
Secret Mountain	CD
INSPIRATION TAPES FOR TEENS	**12+**
Power of Intention	TAPE
Dare to Dream	TAPE
Quality 30 minute tapes in protected cases	
A LITTLE TIME OUT TAPES	**4-100**
Beach Bliss	
Flight Fantasy	
Moonlight Magic	
A Little Time Out CD (Includes the 3 above)	
For individuals or groups aged 5-100	
SCHOOL MASTERY CDs	
Vol 1 For ages 6 -17	CD
Vol 2 For 15+	CD
CHILDREN'S TAPES	**4-10**
Boredom Buster	TAPE
Misery Guts Fixer	TAPE
Customized CDs available on request	
ENDLESS JOURNEY A Message for Every Child Ever Born	

Other Creative Visualizations

Let's Imagine Tapes and CDs

Created by Isabel and David Andrews	***www.magicmusic.com.au***
A Bush Adventure	ages 4-10
A World of Fun and Fantasy	ages 4-10
The Crystal Castle	ages 6-13
A Journey through Time	ages 6-13
Success at Study	teens
Tranquillity	beautiful music for all ages

Created by Petrea King	***www.questforlife.com.au***
Dolphin Magic	
Soar Like an Eagle	
Sleep Easy	

Music I have found to be excellent for calming at home and school:

- ❖ Ken Davis: **Inspiration** Dolphin/ocean sounds
- ❖ Tony O'Connor: **Mariner : Tales of the Wind: Rainforest Magic : Summer Rain : In Touch : Seashore Sunrise : Uluru : Windjana : Australian Bush Garden**
- ❖ Stephen Halpen: **Inner Peace : Spectrum Suite**
- ❖ Will Upson – Albany, Western Australia
- ❖ Red Dot/WA Salvage Various CD's featuring the Seasons and Nature Sounds incl The Mystical Call of the Loon.
- ❖ Baroque Music and some Classical Music.
- ❖ *Any music with a beat slower than the heart beat will calm the energy field. Of course the reverse occurs.*
- ❖ Robert J. Boyd Images and Reflections 1,2,3. Angel Song. Sunset Meditation Available through Robert at his web site www.robertboydmusic.com
- ❖ Paul Gilman (USA) – www.paulgilman.com Emmy-award winning composer.

Aromatherapy Products for Calming:

❖ Lavender, Harmony Plus, Meditation Blend, Relax and Alert.
  Plus many others. (I really recommend the Harmony Plus for
  calming.)
  Available from Leanne Dobson 08 9293 4562
  The Herb Cottage 149 Railway Pde, Gooseberry Hill W.A.
❖ Pure Sandalwood Essence made at Mt Romance ,The
  Sandalwood Factory, Albany WA. Available via mail order.
  08 9841 7788
I thoroughly recommend the gonging experience with the sandalwood
essence before hand…deeply relaxing.

Esteem Plus — Fax to 08 9755 3488   (ABN: 360 368 645 28)

Name: _____ **Date:** _____

Address: _____

_____ **Postcode:** _____

Product	Price	Quantity	Total
Time Out Series quality CDs			
School Mastery #1	$35		
School Mastery #2	$35		
Just a Little Time Out	$35		
Rainbow Balance	$35		
My Safe Place	$35		
Secret Mountain	$35		
Children's Tapes quality 10 minute tapes just for kids aged 4-10			
Boredom Buster	$14.30		
Misery Guts fixer	$14.30		
A Little Time Out quality relaxation tapes for individuals or groups aged 5-100			
Beach Bliss	$14.30		
Flight Fantasy	$14.30		
Moonlight Magic	$14.30		
A Little time Out 3-Pack	$40.00		
		Subtotal	
(Free postage within Australia)		Postage	
		Total	

Authorization Name: _____

Signature: _____

Cash ☐   Cheque ☐   COD ☐   Money Order ☐
Credit Card: VISA ☐   MasterCard ☐   BankCard ☐

Name on card: _____

Card Number: _____

Expiry Date: _____ Amount: $ _____

Signature: _____

Keynote Addresses, Seminars & Programs

Maggie is a member of National Speakers Association of Australia and is a competent, enthusiastic presenter.

She has done presentations nationally and internationally.

Her passion is building awareness and skills to cope with and conquer life. As a Resiliency and Wellness Specialist, Maggie runs seminars and programs in schools, communities and the corporate world.

For more details on these presentations – visit her website:
www.esteemplus.com
or call her mobile: 0418 417 305

Feedback

Making a Real Difference Conference – *Swan Education District Novotel Langley Hotel, Perth.*
"Maggie Dent is an inspiration. I could listen to her all day."
"Maggie Dent was fantastic and related issues everyone was in tune with. A lot of practical ideas - one of the best PD's I 've attended."

Peel Education Conference – *Mandurah Arts Centre July 2001*
"Good use of humour. Used the audience participation well. Great energy!"
"She's very inspiring, what a hoot. I wish she had been my teacher."
"So human and in touch. Power words of wisdom. Touched the heart of why we are here why we are doing what we do. Thank you all."

WA Association of Teacher Assistants Conference – *August 2000 Rendezvous Hotel, Scarborough*
"I have never in my six years of attending WAATA conferences witnessed such an emotional response to a speaker from so many people. The standing ovation at the close of your session was given with so much feeling and I as the person delegated to thank you was left with nothing further needing to be said. Thank you."   Jackie Thomason, Chairperson.

Book Orders- Email to maggiedent@maggiedent.com

One book postage free within Australia!

Orders at applicable rates

Name: _____

School/Organization: _____

Order Nº: _____

Address: _____

Phone: _____

Quantity: _____

Esteem Plus
PO Box 402
Dunsborough
Western Australia 6281

Maggie Dent
quietly improving lives
calmness . simplicity . quiet

Online Resources

Get all the latest information, sign up for seminars, order products online or subscribe to the mailing list to get Maggie's regular newsletter FREE!

www.esteemplus.com

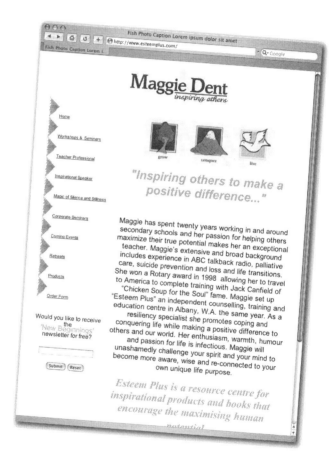

Just One More Day

To my child…

*Just for this morning, I am going to smile when I see your face
and laugh when I feel like crying.*

*Just for this morning, I will let you wake up softly, all rumpled
in your sheets and I will hold you until you are ready for the day.*

*Just for this morning, I will let you choose what you want to wear,
and smile and say how perfect it is.*

*Just for this morning, I am going to step over the laundry, and
pick you up and take you to the park to play.*

*Just for this morning, I will leave the dishes in the sink, and
let you teach me how to put that puzzle of yours together.*

*Just for this afternoon, I will unplug the telephone and keep the
computer off, and sit with you in the back yard and blow bubbles.*

*Just for this afternoon, I will not yell once, not even a tiny grumble
when you scream and whine for the ice cream truck, and I will buy you
one if he comes by.*

*Just for this afternoon, I won't worry about what you are going to
be when you grow up, or second guess every decision I have made
where you are concerned.*

*Just for this afternoon, I will let you help me bake cookies, and
I won't stand over you trying to fix them.*

*Just for this afternoon, I will take you to McDonald's and buy us
both a Happy Meal so you can have both toys.*

*Just for this evening, I will hold you in my arms and tell you a
story about how you were born, and how much I love you.*

*Just for this evening, I will let you splash in the tub and not get
angry.*

*Just for this evening, I will let you stay up late while we sit on
the porch and count all the stars.*

*Just for this evening, I will snuggle beside you for hours, and miss
my favorite TV show.*

*Just for this evening, when I run my fingers through your hair as you
pray, I will simply be grateful that God has given me the greatest gift
ever given.*

*I will think about the mothers who are searching for their missing
children, the mothers who are visiting their children's graves instead
of their bedrooms, and mothers who are in hospital rooms watching their
children suffer senselessly, and screaming inside that they can't handle
it anymore, and when I kiss you goodnight, I will hold you a little
tighter, a little longer.*

*It is then that I will thank God for you, and ask him for nothing,
except one more day.*

Author Unknown